In the World but
Not of It

In the World but
Not of It

New Teachings from Jesus on
Embodying the Divine

GINA LAKE

Endless Satsang Foundation

www.RadicalHappiness.com

Cover photo: © Supershabashnyi /iStock.com

ISBN: 978-1517739904

To the Christ in everyone.

Contents

INTRODUCTION

I, the one you have known as Jesus the Christ, am writing this, another book, through this scribe, Gina Lake, to assist you in living the teachings I gave so long ago. These teachings have nothing to do with religion, rules, or commandments, but with transcending the need for such things and, instead, living from the wellspring of your being, which knows how to move in this world in perfect grace, peace, and love.

This wellspring is what I will call Christ Consciousness, although there are many names for it in various spiritual traditions. It is called Buddha nature in Buddhism, Atman in Hinduism, and the Self in Advaita Vedanta. In spiritual circles, it is called Presence, Essence, Stillness, true self, or simply Consciousness, to name but a few of the terms.

"Christ Consciousness," as I am using it, points to the divinity within everyone and the potential for that divinity to become a living reality, to become what lives you. I was an example of that possibility in my lifetime two thousand years ago. "I and my Father are one" expresses this.

This is an advanced teaching and not for everyone. Some still require the rules and commandments to keep the ego in check. They need an external authority to guide their behavior. This was especially true two thousand years ago, when humanity was still in its infancy and less evolved than it is today.

But now, many are ready for the Christ within to come forward and manifest in the world more fully. The birthing of *this* Christ—of Christ Consciousness—is the true second coming. You are to be witnesses to this birth within yourself and others. This is an important and special time on earth.

Christ Consciousness is within everyone, whether they recognize me as a master or not and whether they recognize that potential within themselves or not. What I came to teach in that incarnation so long ago was this: The consciousness that is within me is also within you. You are the son as equally as I am. You are the "I am" I spoke of. You and I are one. You and everyone else are one.

There is only one consciousness with infinitely many unique manifestations. Each is an expression of love from that which gave birth to them, whether you call that God/Goddess, the Father/Mother, Oneness, the Divine, Allah, Spirit, Source, the Formless, the Tao, the Great Spirit, the Nameless, or the Unmanifest. There are many names for what is behind all life and which cannot be understood by the mind or expressed in words.

By imagining this mysterious force of creation as an individual—as a god or a Father—it is made manageable for the mind. But any concept of God cannot begin to touch the reality of God, which can only be experienced, never understood.

When you are experiencing God, to the extent that is possible as a human being, you are experiencing Christ Consciousness. God lives within you, and you experience that as a particular state of consciousness, a state of being. Although often obscured, this "state" is not a passing state, like other states of consciousness, but always present and available. Although Christ Consciousness may seem to be an experience or a state of consciousness, it is actually *what* is conscious. It is the experience of Christ alive in you, as you.

Two thousand years ago, I came to show you how to *be* peace and love and ultimately to bring those to this world. I taught by example and through other means what it is like to live in Christ Consciousness. My message was misunderstood by many then and distorted by many others since then. But today, people are more ready for this message and more able to understand it and embody it than ever before.

So in this book, I will speak to you using today's language and terms, and I will build upon what others have taught since, for the truth that I taught has been taught by many others throughout history and is being taught today by many more than ever before.

The truth I am speaking of is the truth about who you are — about your human *and* divine nature, for you are equally both. You are as divine as you perceive me to be. And, for now, you are also human. You walk with one foot in the world of form and another in the Formless. You are a bridge between the two. This mysterious duality within your being is what this book is about.

I want to speak with you intimately about this, as a brother, as a friend, as one who has lived this duality. And, yes, I will speak as a teacher too, but not as someone who is above you, not as someone who is more godlike than you, but someone who is no different than you.

This is blasphemy to some, but only to those who do not understand the truth hidden in your scriptures. It was not my intention to be made into a god. That was not why I came, and I did not make myself into a god. I came to show you the beauty of your own soul and what is possible as a human. I came to show you that it is possible to be both human and divine, to be love incarnate.

Many worship me, for they see me as the embodiment of love, but that love is equally in you. What I have come to teach now is that you can embody love, as I did. You can become Christ within this human life and learn to embody all that is good within you.

This is no small task, but many of you are up to it and want this more than anything else. To reunite with your divine self, such a drive and longing are essential. Although this Homecoming is everyone's destiny, the journey is long and arduous, and for such journeys a trusted guide is useful and often necessary.

This book is but one external guide. The truest guide rests in your Heart, and any true outer guide knows this and points you to that. My task is to point you to your own inner wisdom, to the Christ within, which is trustworthy, patient, generous, courageous, loving, and compassionate.

Every good quality is already yours as part of your divine inheritance. And yet, something else is here as well that veils your innate goodness and causes suffering. We will examine this aspect of your humanity—the ego—so that you can more easily overcome this obstacle to realizing your divinity.

Religion often paints worldly life as something to be transcended or endured before returning to heaven. But if the kingdom of heaven is within, as I taught, then returning to heaven means returning to Christ Consciousness, which has been temporarily lost or hidden by the human condition, more specifically, by the ego and associated conditioning. This return to heaven happens while in the body—while in the world—not after leaving the body.

Embodiment refers to the possibility of embodying the divine self within the human form, of embodying the Formless while in form, of being in the world but not of it. It offers the possibility of enjoying heaven on earth and being in joy in this life. It is each and everyone's destiny to find joy in this physical existence.

Being human is not essentially problematic. It is a gift to be human, to be able to have experiences as a sentient being on this plane of existence. It is an adventure your soul, and God through you, has willingly embarked upon. And like all good adventures, this one has a very big challenge to overcome, and that is the ego. It was designed to be a stumbling block to reclaiming heaven and the love, peace, and happiness that is your divine inheritance. It is also part of a perfect plan to bring you Home.

The ego is what makes life the drama and adventure that it is. The ego is the source of human suffering and the only thing veiling your divine nature. This suffering, however, is also what awakens you from the ego's nightmare. The heroic journey, as I have written about elsewhere, in *A Heroic Life*, is the vanquishing of the ego, or putting it in its rightful place, and the clearing away of the obscurations to Christ Consciousness. Once these are cleared to some extent, the light of the divine self can shine through. So let us begin by examining the nature of the obscurations, or clouds, that block the light of divine Consciousness.

Jesus, dictated to Gina Lake
January, 2016

CHAPTER 1

The Clouds

The Illusion Spun by Thoughts

The obscurations to Christ Consciousness, to experiencing your divine nature, are simply thoughts. These thoughts are the ones that flow continually through your mind, speaking to you as if they were you, an authority figure, or a friend. They are primarily about you and your life, what to do, how to be, what happened, and what will be. I will be referring to this mental commentary as the thought-stream, the voice in your head, or the egoic mind. I am not referring to thoughts that belong to the intellect, or the rational aspect of the mind.

Imagine that: Something as flimsy and ephemeral as a stream of thoughts is powerful enough to hide your divine nature from you and, in its place, create a sense of yourself as separate, limited, vulnerable, and lacking. Thoughts create the illusion of a self that has problems, fears, desires, struggles, emotions, and pain. They create the false self. Without thoughts, problems and suffering disappear and so does the false self. Thoughts perform quite a magic trick!

Thoughts couldn't perform this magic unless they were also compelling, interesting, seemingly true, and most importantly, seemingly *yours*. Thoughts aren't just thoughts—they seem like *your* thoughts. They seem to be personal. As a result, they are fascinating and important to *you*. Without your thoughts, after all, who would you be?

People cling to their thoughts as if for dear life, and rightfully so, because without them, there would be no one with a life story, no past, no future, not even a name. Without your thoughts about yourself, you would be no one, nothing. You would be just this, just Christ Consciousness, just what is looking out of your eyes and experiencing life. And that's what you actually are: You are what is experiencing life right here and now without any mental commentary.

You are just this that is reading these words and just this that can determine the truth of them. The egoic mind might agree, disagree, or bring confusion to what you are reading, but those are just more thoughts. Without those thoughts, there's either an *experience* of truth or not, or of whatever else you might be experiencing through your senses.

As you progress spiritually, the thoughts in the thought-stream become less compelling, less interesting, less true, and less yours. You come to see that you aren't actually responsible for those thoughts. This evolution in one's relationship to thoughts makes detaching from them eventually possible. As thoughts are seen to be less personal, they're easier to let go of or leave alone. They can come and go in the background without affecting you, because you understand they are simply the programming common to all humans and not uniquely yours. You see that your thoughts actually have nothing to do with you and mean nothing about you—the real you, that is—although they have everything to do with the false self.

This evolution in relationship to thoughts can also be described as moving from believing yourself to be the thinker of thoughts to knowing yourself as the experiencer of thoughts and of everything else arising in the moment. You come to see that you are the spacious, silent Presence in which thoughts, feelings, desires, sense impressions, intuitions, knowing, insights, inspiration, and motivations come and go. You are the ground of being out of which everything you experience arises. You are that which is eternal and untouched by the coming and going of thoughts, feelings, desires, sense impressions, and the whole world of form. And yet, there is total love for form and for its coming and going. What a miracle this world is! In Christ Consciousness, you are in love with life itself and with every way that life manifests.

As thoughts lose their stickiness and the sense that they belong to you, they also lose their ability to shape your perceptions or result in unpleasant feelings. Freedom from thoughts, and to some extent feelings, is the state of enlightenment, the state of being in the world joyfully but not of the world. When thoughts are experienced as just thoughts and nothing more, Christ Consciousness can shine through you. Then *it* becomes what moves, what speaks, and what chooses.

Going from attachment to and belief in thoughts to nonattachment and non-belief is generally a lengthy process. This spiritual process can take years, decades, or lifetimes, depending on one's level of spiritual development and other factors. Those who seem to attain enlightenment overnight have laid the groundwork for that over many lifetimes of spiritual practice and encountering spiritual teachings. Thoughts don't give up their hold easily. The ego, which is behind the thought-stream, has a firm grip on humanity, and the ego and the thoughts and feelings it generates don't suddenly disappear overnight.

The illusion spun by thoughts—what Hindus call *maya*—must be seen through again and again in each moment, until eventually your thoughts give way enough to reveal what is true and real: your divine nature. Once there is some space between thoughts and some capacity to witness thought, the illusion begins to break down, and your divine nature begins to shine through. This is the process we are going to examine and get to know more intimately: How do humans go from ego domination to embodying their divine radiance?

Thoughts Are Like Clouds

Buddhists often liken true nature, or Christ Consciousness, to a clear, cloudless sky, and thoughts, which create *maya* and the false self, as clouds in this sky. I can think of no better analogy than this, so I will borrow it and elaborate on it. The clear, cloudless sky, like divine nature, is always there, whether there are clouds or not. It is pristine, ever-present, immutable, and untouched by the clouds that pass through it.

The clouds, or thoughts, on the other hand, are forever changing and forever coming and going. Thoughts never stay the same for long. Although certain thoughts arise repeatedly, no one thought lasts more than a few seconds unless it's given attention. Like clouds, thoughts are filmy and unsubstantial, constantly morphing into something else, and have a limited lifespan.

Just as there are different kinds of clouds, there are different kinds of thoughts. Some are like pretty, puffy, white clouds that dot the sky and interfere little with the sunshine. These might be happy or positive thoughts, neutral or objective thoughts, functional thoughts, or previously problematic thoughts that are no longer believed. They interfere little with enjoying life because your attention doesn't get stuck on them, and so they don't result in unpleasant emotions. They tend to come and go quickly without leaving a trace and without blocking the joy, peace, love, and gratitude of your true nature.

Most thoughts in the thought-stream, however, are more like gray or overcast clouds that fill the sky so totally that it's as if there is no sky. Such thoughts can change your perception of the world so completely that your perception *becomes* your reality. Then the brilliant radiance of your divine self doesn't even seem to exist. Such thoughts change your experience of life in the same way colored glasses do, but they're more like dirty or distorted lenses. These are negative or limiting thoughts, fearful thoughts, angry thoughts, sad and regretful thoughts, and other emotionally laden thoughts as well as strong opinions and any other thoughts that are deeply believed but not completely true.

Thoughts in general, especially dark ones, can so capture your attention and create such a convincing story and emotional experience that you lose touch with the whole truth about a situation, and the wisdom, joy, peace, love, courage, and other qualities of your divine self seem lost or inaccessible. But fortunately, the mind doesn't have to be completely clear of thoughts to experience your divine self. It only has to be clear enough for the light of Christ Consciousness to get through a little.

This sky analogy also works for describing the thinning, or weakening, of the ego that occurs with spiritual progress over many lifetimes or sometimes in just one. The person who is ego identified and deeply involved with the thought-stream lives in a world of thick, mostly gray, clouds. If the egoic trance is strong enough, that person might not even realize there is a sky, or experience it only rarely. Those moments when the sky is experienced are felt to be peak or very special and magical moments, which is how Christ Consciousness feels in contrast to egoic consciousness.

When someone begins to realize the existence of the sky, they're beginning to awaken out of egoic consciousness. Once someone has had enough glimpses of blue-sky consciousness, the desire to experience that more often is ignited. Then the search begins for the means of achieving that.

The means are spiritual practices, such as meditation, contemplation, prayer, and inquiry, as well as psychological methods, such as emotional healing, affirmations, and positive thinking. Many of these practices and methods dissolve attachment to the thoughts in the thought-stream by exposing them as untrue, limiting, and not useful. Other methods reprogram the mind to be more neutral or positive, which is also helpful.

As a result of these practices and methods and other spiritual catalysts, which result in more frequent experiences of Presence, the clouds—the ego and its thoughts, drives, fears, and other negative emotions—thin and become more translucent, less solid and real. With continued practices, the clouds transform from thick, dark, and sometimes ominous to thin, white, and lovely, with blue sky showing through most days. Eventually what remains in the thought-stream are mostly thoughts that coexist harmoniously within the sky without blocking it. Those thoughts are allowed to come and go, to move through the sky naturally.

And yet, an even more brilliant sky is possible once the puffy, white clouds also disappear, since the positive and neutral thoughts are not needed either. Most of those are simply commentary about what you already know and what's already happening. To function, you don't even need those thoughts, although it might seem like you do. Christ Consciousness moves beautifully in life without the thoughts in the thought-stream. If you need to think to perform some task, you think, but otherwise thoughts are not required.

Nevertheless, even for those who are self-realized or awakened, the absolutely clear blue sky of a totally clear mind is usually only temporary, as some white clouds and occasionally dark ones—some sticky thoughts and tumultuous feelings—revisit periodically. When that happens, the person who is self-realized knows that the blue sky is what's real and permanent and that the dark clouds will pass. This knowledge helps enormously in maintaining a sense of blue sky even in the midst of dark clouds.

At every stage of the spiritual journey, some amount of ego remains. In the beginning, the ego is thicker and holds more sway. It isn't always recognized and is still often identified with. As the journey progresses and there's more awareness of the ego, it becomes thinner, more transparent, less substantial, and less powerful. But it is still there. The ego continues to thin until there's only the barest amount, only enough to function.

The ego is generally the thinnest when people are by themselves, and most apparent when they're interacting with others. Then thoughts inevitably roll in. If those thoughts are seen for what they are, useless and unnecessary, they remain as wisps and quickly dissipate. Then even in one's interactions, Christ Consciousness can shine through. However, if those thoughts are identified with a little, they become puffy white clouds, and some Presence is lost. If they are identified with a lot, they become thicker and possibly gray, as they turn into the stories people tell, which make them unhappy. Then the ego is back in charge. If the stories are identified with intensely enough, they create feelings and cover over the blue sky completely, at least for a time.

Most people are identified with their thought-stream most of the time, with only brief moments of clear seeing and freedom from their thoughts. For those who are self-realized, or awakened, the opposite is true: They live in blue-sky consciousness and move into some degree of identification with thought briefly and then return to blue-sky consciousness. Those who've realized that they are the blue sky never lose touch with blue-sky consciousness. Even when they're identified with egoic thoughts, they never completely forget their true nature.

What causes even those who are self-realized to temporarily lose touch with their true nature are any remaining egoic thoughts that are still believed and the feelings connected to them. The thoughts that continue to linger in the thought-stream are most likely ones tied to emotional wounds that haven't been fully digested and healed. There may also be some remaining egoic tendencies, such as the need to judge or be right.

Although the strength of egoic thoughts and tendencies naturally weakens over time as a result of simply being aware of them without identifying with them, they don't necessarily completely go away. Even after conditioning has been seen through quite thoroughly, some emotional residue usually remains, which can be reactivated under the right circumstances. When conditioning does get triggered, that's when more about it can be discovered and healed if you're willing to question and investigate those thoughts and feelings. How this is done will be explained more fully later.

The Kinds of Thoughts in the Thought-Stream

So far, I've been describing how the mind gradually becomes clearer with spiritual progress. Let's take a look now at the kinds of thoughts that need to be cleared away for Christ Consciousness to shine through. In other words, let's take a look at the nature of the clouds.

The thought-stream is full of thoughts—clouds—generated by the ego to serve the ego. The ego is a cloud-producing machine, designed to obscure reality, including your divine nature, and create a virtual reality of sorts, one that serves the ego's needs and drives. The thought-stream is nearly always the voice of the ego.

Take this in a moment, because this is not an overstatement: The voice in your head is nearly always the voice of the ego. A part of you doesn't want to believe this, because this is a very radical idea, and believing it will change your life. Spiritual truth is radical. It changes your reality. But since you are reading this, you must be ready to question consensus reality.

Becoming aware of the various types of thoughts in the thought-stream will help you get to know your ego. This is the first step in weakening the ego, the false self, or in other words, thinning out the clouds. Recognizing egoic thoughts when they arise and not agreeing with them or taking those thoughts on as your own produces a break in the clouds, enabling you to begin to live in blue-sky consciousness and to embody Christ Consciousness.

Most of the thoughts in the thought-stream describe someone. If you believe those thoughts, they become your identity. The false self is created by thoughts that have "I" in them: "I'm the pretty one." "I never get a fair chance." "I'll never be happy." "I never get anything right." "I'm such a klutz." "I'm smarter than most." "I always come out on top." "I can't trust anyone." "I'll never find love."

Such ideas are never completely true, many of them make you feel bad, and all of them color and distort reality and often become self-fulfilling prophecies. And yet, people accept these thoughts as the truth about themselves, as if these ideas *are* who they are. But these self-descriptions only describe the false self. They're simply the clothing their false self generally wears or is wearing at a particular time.

The trouble with these ideas, besides the obvious, is that when you are experiencing yourself as the false self, you're not experiencing your true self, your divine self. In any moment, you are experiencing one or the other. People go back and forth between the two, although most of the time, most are identified with the false self. More elegantly, this could be described as a dance between the false self and the true self, as one or the other is identified with in any given moment.

To experience yourself as the true self, you have to first let go of experiencing yourself as the false self. This is a matter of letting go of or not giving your attention to the thoughts in the thought-stream that are responsible for creating the false self. To this end, it is useful to be aware of the types of thoughts that support the false self.

Thoughts that uphold the false self:

1. **Thoughts pertaining to "I," including thoughts about other people in relation to you.** Although such thoughts seem integral to life, they actually aren't needed to function. They're only integral to the life of the false self.

2. **Thoughts that attempt to make you better or less than someone else or ones that make you right and others wrong.** These include judgments, criticisms, blame, fault-finding, and comparisons. These types of thoughts are designed to fortify the false self.

3. **Thoughts that assume or pretend to know something with absolute certainty.** These include opinions, beliefs, and many of the thoughts about other people. These also strengthen the false self.

4. **Fears and worries.** These always come from the ego and never from the divine self.

5. **Doubts, self-doubts, confusion, and indecision.** Knowing, or clarity, naturally arises when knowing is needed and not before then. So when you feel confused or don't know something but you want to, that's the ego.

6. **Thoughts about the past.** These rarely serve the moment but take you out of Presence. More often, they serve the ego's agenda of storytelling.

7. **Thoughts and fantasies about the future, including compulsive planning.** These also rarely serve the moment but take you out of Presence. They're the ego's attempt at getting a better now. But the future never arrives; it is only always now.

8. **Black and white thinking and ideas of good and bad, right and wrong.** Life is not as simple as this type of thinking presumes, although the ego would like it to be. The ego likes to name, categorize, put in a box, and wrap

things up in a tidy bow. This is how it pretends to know things. The ego doesn't think in shades of gray.

9. **Thoughts related to lacking or needing something, the sense that something is missing, wanting things to be different, feeling bored, complaining.** A sense of lack and the fear and desire stirred up by that drive the ego to do what it does. But lack is imagined and just a concept, a belief that something is missing, when nothing is. Everything simply is as it is and the only way it can be for the time being.

10. **Thoughts that push you to be constantly doing something, a feeling of restlessness, the need for constant mental stimulation.** If you were to slow down and not keep yourself and your mind so busy, you might experience your divine self, and that would diminish the ego's power. To stay in power, the ego has to keep you busy and absorbed in the world of thoughts.

11. **Thoughts designed to stir up emotions or create drama.** The ego loves problems and drama because they give the false self something to do and a way to feel important—to feel like somebody, even if that's somebody whose life is a mess. There's no better way to create drama and problems than by stirring up emotions.

12. **Thoughts that contain "should" and other demands to be a certain way,** as if a parent or other authority figure is commanding you and passing judgment on you. Such thoughts come from the superego, which is formed in childhood to keep the ego in check. But the superego is simply another form of ego.

Becoming familiar with the thoughts in your thought-stream is essential in freeing yourself from them. In service to this, take a moment to write down some of your thoughts. Can you find any that don't come from the ego? Then look at those thoughts more closely to see what your ego is up to:

What is your ego up to? Is it . . .

Trying to be right?

Trying to be in control by pretending to know?

Trying to be better than others?

Trying to measure up when you don't believe you do?

Trying to fix the past?

Trying to get a good future or be secure and safe in the future?

Trying to make yourself small to maintain a negative self-image or to be nonthreatening to others?

Trying to impress others to gain respect or something else?

Trying to be nice to get love or something else from others?

Trying to manipulate others in other ways to get what you want?

Trying to fix other people to feel good about yourself or to feel better than others?

Trying to get help or sympathy or create drama by complaining?

Trying to quiet the superego by getting it right and being perfect?

Subtle Ways the Ego Hides

The ego always has an agenda. That agenda may be glaringly apparent or quite subtle and hidden. When the ego is blatantly behaving jealously, greedily, manipulatively, selfishly, insensitively, judgmentally, arrogantly, angrily, tyrannically, or in any other of its usual ways, spotting it is easy. However, as people advance spiritually and become more aware of the ego, its tactics get more subtle. The ego lives on, even after you've caught on to its most obvious manifestations. You can never assume you're finished with the ego. If you examine your thoughts closely, you'll see that the ego is still there in some form in the thought-stream.

Even in the most spiritually advanced people, the ego can reemerge. One of the ways it does this is by twisting, corrupting, or co-opting the positive feelings and insights that naturally arise from your divine self. For instance, the ego can, in an instant, turn a deep insight into a judgment or use that insight to try to make you right or superior. The ego may show up in your tone of voice while sharing that insight or simply in your need to share that insight. Listen to yourself as you share any insights and see if you can hear the ego, or ask yourself, "Why do I feel a need to share this insight? Is it really helpful to do that now?"

A similar thing can happen with other gifts, or qualities, of the divine self:

Gratitude can easily slide into an egoic high, gloating, or bragging.

Joy can slide into insensitivity to other people's pain.

Peace can slide into complacency and self-satisfaction.

Love can become prideful about being loving and good, as an identity forms around that.

The ego also tends to turn spiritual experiences or expanded states into a new identity it's proud of: "I'm awake," it proclaims inwardly or even to others. Anything you say about "I" is bound to have some ego in it.

Here are some examples of thoughts that often go through people's minds, which are subtle or not so subtle expressions of ego:

Examples of the ego's judgments disguised as questions or observations:

He sure likes to eat! (implying he eats too much).

I don't understand why she does that (implying her behavior is abnormal or strange).

What is going on with that (implying something is silly or stupid)?

He's being so nice today (implying that is unusual).

Examples of the ego needing to be right or thinking it knows better than someone else:

I told you so!

I can't stand to see him wasting his life like that.

She didn't do what I told her to do.

That's what happens when....

He never listens to me (implying he should, because I'm right).

She doesn't know a thing about handling money (implying you do).

Examples of the ego pretending to know by predicting the future or mindreading:

If I don't get that job, I'll never find another one.

I'm going to hate getting together with them.

He is perfect for me.

He's a snob.

She thinks she's smarter than me.

He's going to have a heart attack if he keeps doing that.

Examples of the ego creating a sense of lack:

This day wasn't very interesting.

I'll be happy when....

I wish I had a more exciting life.

Why does everyone else seem to be able to find a relationship?

I'm just not as smart as he is.

I could have done better.

It's so cold today.

I wish I had a new rug.

I didn't get enough exercise today.

My sister never calls.

Degrees of Identification

Complete belief and complete disbelief are not the only possibilities when it comes to your thoughts. There are shades of belief. You may believe a thought just a little or a lot. Or you may believe a thought for a second or for a lifetime. How strongly and for how long you believe a thought makes all the difference in how much that thought affects your experience of life and how much you suffer as a result of it. So it's not so much the thoughts themselves that cause suffering, since people generally have very similar thoughts, but how deeply someone is identified with those thoughts and for how long. By identification, I mean how much time is spent involved with a thought, how deeply it is believed, and whether it is given voice to and acted on.

There's one important caveat to the statement that people generally have similar thoughts: Those who've been abused, neglected, or traumatized usually have many more negative thoughts than those who haven't had these experiences. For those with particularly negative minds, the thought-stream will need to become more positive and neutral before detaching from thoughts is possible. This can be accomplished through psychotherapy and other healing methods.

There will always be some degree of identification when you're busy doing things and interacting with people. This is not a problem if identification is very brief. The longer you believe a thought, however, the more likely it will turn into a story, and then an emotion, and then more stories, and then more emotions. Then those emotions are acted on, often compulsively, destructively, or unwisely. That's when a thought becomes a problem.

Here's an example to illustrate this. Let's say the thought is: "I'll never get another job I like." That's a story, meaning an assumption or conclusion about you and your life. Stories are never completely true, although they usually have some truth to them. You know you're telling a story when it makes you feel bad.

If you believe the story "I'll never get another job I like," you'll feel bad. When you feel bad, you think more negative thoughts, which stir up even more negative feelings. Then you might cope with those feelings by eating too much or indulging in other destructive behaviors, such as compulsive shopping, sleeping all day, taking drugs, endlessly watching mind-numbing TV shows, and so on.

Such thoughts, feelings, and activities undermine any motivation that would put you back in the job market and make you an attractive employee. You might miss opportunities that life is offering because you aren't open to or available for them. Thus, a story such as "I'll never find another job I like" can become a self-fulfilling prophecy. In other words, your thoughts and feelings can create the experience described by your thoughts and feelings.

The more beliefs you have that are uninvestigated and unconscious, the more identified with them you'll be, and the more they'll affect your emotional state, your behavior, and consequently your life. People have uninvestigated thoughts because built into thoughts is the sense that they are true, so people automatically assume that what they think is true. But this kind of certainty and other strong convictions and opinions are not a sign of truth or inner strength, but a sign of a strong ego. The ego believes in its beliefs and opinions. This is one of the ways the false self is maintained.

If you weren't programmed to automatically believe your thoughts, you'd be able to see the truth about the thought-stream and the ego much more easily. But life doesn't make this that easy to see! Human beings are programmed to believe thoughts that lead them astray and make them unhappy. What a dilemma!

The suffering that comes from believing the thought-stream eventually motivates people to question their thoughts, and then they discover the truth about them. Life gives you an ego that delivers suffering, but it also gives you a way out of suffering: awareness and investigation. What is capable of seeing the truth is, of course, your divine self, since that's actually the only thing here. The ego, or false self, is just a bunch of thoughts, and those thoughts are meant to ensnare you, not reveal the truth.

How to Tell When You Are Ego Identified

It isn't that difficult to tell when you're identified with the ego. There are certain telltale signs. If you can recognize the ego in a thought before you identify with that thought, that's even better. However, as we've seen, many thoughts that appear quite neutral have the ego driving them and hiding in them, and those might still catch you up.

Identifying with thoughts that have little ego in them is not much of a problem. Believing a thought that has a lot of ego in it is another story. Those types of thoughts, if not obvious to you, will be obvious to others and likely to trigger their own egos. For example, if you were to say to your partner, "I ended up being right about that," your partner just might agree with you, even though your ego is getting the best of you in that moment, albeit subtly. Only the ego cares about being right and will use any opportunity to score a point. But if instead of that you said, "You really blew it," those words just might start a fight in which your partner points out all the times *you* "blew it." Those words have much more ego in them.

The tone of the voice in your head and of your own voice when speaking to others and the language used has a lot to do with whether a statement activates your ego or someone else's. Thoughts or words that are emotionally charged, such as "You really blew it," are bound to elicit negative feelings, much more so than a more objective comment. This applies to your internal self-talk as well. If you say to yourself, "I really blew it," that has a much greater chance of making you feel bad and for longer than "I ended up being wrong about that." What you say to yourself and how you say it really matters.

Many have learned over the years to talk to themselves more kindly and objectively, and that keeps the negative ego in check. You can train the voice in your head to be more positive, neutral, and friendly by not listening to or identifying with it when it's negative and unkind. If you work with it, the voice in your head can become more benevolent. But you don't need that benevolent voice either. You don't need the voice in your head at all.

The most obvious sign that you're ego identified is emotional reactivity and negative feelings, such as fear, anger, hurt, jealousy, envy, or hatred. When such feelings arise, you've become your ego, even if only briefly. The more you engage in the thoughts that produced those feelings, the longer those feelings will last and the more powerful a hold they'll have on you.

The strength of your negative feelings is a measure of how strongly, and possibly how long, you've bought into a belief or story. Those feelings, in turn, convince you there's a reason to feel that way—otherwise why would you feel that intensely? The answer is, you feel that way because you believe your thoughts, not because your thoughts are true. Your feelings convince you that your thoughts are true, even when they aren't. People don't realize that their thoughts are what make them feel the way they do, not circumstances. The ego uses circumstances to create feelings by telling a story about those circumstances, and that story makes you feel bad.

If, for example, you believe the thought "I'm going to be homeless," you'll feel terrified. Those feelings of terror convince you that becoming homeless must be a real possibility, without realizing you feel alarmed because you believed that thought, not because that thought is true. The mind just makes things up. It doesn't have a crystal ball.

The strength of a feeling is a measure only of how strongly and frequently you have believed a thought, not of a thought's veracity. Any thought that's entertained frequently will seem true because it will produce feelings that make it seem true. Furthermore, if a thought is entertained often enough, it will become habitual, and the resulting feelings will become habitual. For example, if you give angry thoughts your attention, you'll create a habit of thinking those thoughts. Then your anger will also become habitual and easily and automatically triggered.

People do this with grief as well. As normal as it is to grieve over a loss, many magnify and extend their grief unnecessarily by focusing on sad thoughts and returning to them repeatedly. Then thinking such thoughts becomes habitual, and the feelings become habitual. Eliminating this pattern from the neural circuits will take a concerted effort to discontinue the habit, as it does with any habit.

Negative feelings are the most obvious sign the ego is in play, but you can also assume you're ego identified whenever you feel contracted. This manifests as a sense of contraction in your body and feeling tense, tight, stressed, restless, out of balance, irritable, annoyed, or dissatisfied. You might feel on edge, like you want to pick a fight. Or when the contraction is extreme, you might feel like giving up or curling up in a ball. More often than not, negative feelings and a sense of contraction go hand in hand.

The opposite of contraction is feeling peace, ease, contentment, relaxation, gratitude, joy, and a sense of being in the flow or being lost in what you're doing. These are the hallmarks of the divine self. If you aren't feeling this way, you're involved with the ego to some extent. The degree to which you are ego identified is the degree to which you lack peace and contentment and feel dissatisfied and ill at ease.

You are always receiving feedback from your divine self about how aligned you are with it. It tells you through a sense of contraction or expansion and through positive and negative feelings whether or not you're in ego and just how much. The divine self is always communicating with the human self and doing what it can to bring the human self into alignment with it, while simultaneously honoring your free will to choose to be ego identified.

Being very present to your energetic, emotional, and bodily experience will tell you just how identified you are with the ego. Once you realize you're ego identified, you can get curious about how you got caught. What thoughts were you thinking? What beliefs or self-identities were you believing? Do you want to keep feeling this way? When you have enough awareness to stop and ask these questions, then you have a choice: go back into identification or become more present.

The antidote to the suffering caused by ego identification is to turn your attention away from the thought-stream to your present moment experience: what you are seeing, hearing, feeling, and sensing physically and more subtly. Doing this will bring you out of the mind and back into your body and senses. This is where you want to stay, because the body and senses are a doorway into Presence, into Christ Consciousness. From there, life is experienced very differently.

Whenever you drop out of the mind into the body and senses and into Presence, the reward is peace, contentment, gratitude, love, and joy. The trick is to stay in the body and senses long enough to drop into Presence and then to stay in Presence long enough to get enough of a taste to want to stay there. The more familiar you become with Presence, the more the voice in your head loses its attraction.

Finally, another clue that you're ego identified is the subtle pleasure you get from being right, feeling superior, being selfish or unkind, complaining, judging, blaming, or doing any of the other things the ego pushes you to do. On some level, it feels good to be bad. Saying what the ego wants you to say provides some pleasure, some satisfaction. At the very least, the pressure to say it is relieved once it is spoken. The ego's way is the path of least resistance. As such, it is often irresistible.

However, the pleasure you get from indulging the ego is a double-edged sword, because feeling superior, being selfish or unkind, complaining, judging, blaming, and doing the other things the ego does to get this fleeting pleasure ultimately doesn't feel good and doesn't have good results. You feel bad about yourself when you do things that make others feel bad. This is the meaning of "Whatsoever you have done to the least of my brethren, you have done to me." What you do to others, you also do to yourself:

> *When you judge others, you are also hurting yourself, because you can't be judgmental and be happy.*

> *When you are unkind to others, you are also being unkind to yourself, because you can't be unkind and be happy.*

> *When you don't forgive someone, you are also harming yourself by holding hatred inside.*

Whenever you are in ego, you not only hurt others, but also yourself. That's how people learn to not be in ego. This lesson is built into life, and it is how life brings you back home to love.

Being at peace, being content, and being loving and in harmony with others is what feels good. The ego takes you away from this peaceful state, from what you really want. Becoming sensitive to how you're getting pleasure from hurting others and also hurting yourself when you're doing that will help you make another choice.

From this chapter, you might conclude that thoughts are a problem. But only when thoughts cause you to lose touch with your divine self are they a problem. Your *relationship* to thought is what changes with spiritual progress, not so much whether thoughts are running through your mind or not. As you dis-identify with your thoughts, the thought-stream becomes increasingly quiet and neutral or benign. You can and may still be involved with some of your thoughts and even speak them, but you won't believe them to the degree you once did.

When you don't take your thoughts, especially the "I" thoughts, so seriously, as if they were personally true, they lose their fascination along with their bite. Then they can just be there, like the clouds or any other thing that belongs to this world of form. Thoughts are part of life as a human being, and once the truth about them is seen, they're no longer a problem.

Now let's turn our attention to the mysterious duality behind the human condition. Are you human or divine? Yes!

Chapter 2

Duality

Perfect Imperfection

You are both human and divine. You are divine perfection expressing as human imperfection, which itself is perfect. You were perfectly designed to be imperfect! Human imperfections are an intentional part of your design and will always be with you to some extent.

Human imperfections stem largely from the ego, which is an essential aspect of being human that never completely disappears. The ego is not a mistake. It is meant to be part of the human experience. However, it is also intended that you evolve from expressing the ego to expressing your divine nature, while retaining some remnant of ego.

These imperfections are the things you might judge about yourself and others. These are also things that cause suffering, such as the tendency to judge, to be unkind, to gossip, to be jealous or envious, to want to be right, to want attention, to try to control others, to compulsively think, to be addicted, to pretend to know, to be selfish or greedy, to blame, to be unaware of or insensitive to other people's needs and feelings, to be prejudiced, to be ignorant, to argue and compete with others—all the things you might be acknowledging when you shrug your shoulders and say, "I'm only human."

Because these human tendencies cause problems and pain, most people would prefer they didn't have them. And although your natural evolution is towards greater kindness, empathy, peace, love, wisdom, and other qualities of your true nature, which is perfect, as a human being, you will never reach such perfection—and you aren't meant to. To express the perfection of your divine self, the human self doesn't have to be perfect.

One of the most important messages I have to offer you is that it's okay for you to be imperfect. It's okay for you to be human, and it's impossible for you to be other than the way you are right now, although you will most certainly continue to evolve and become more Christ-like.

You may imagine that I was perfect and hold this up as a model, but you shouldn't be surprised if you or others don't live up to this imagined ideal. I was not perfect either. To some, this must sound like blasphemy. But it is hurtful to you and misleading for you to believe that you or anyone else can become a perfect human being. You can and will become a vehicle for expressing Christ Consciousness in the world, but you will still have some human imperfections.

As long as you are human, there will be some degree of pull from your programming into fear, anger, judgment, blame, hatred, self-doubt, jealousy, revenge, dissatisfaction, greed, and other human emotions and tendencies. The programming that makes you human is powerfully controlling. Until people begin to question their thoughts, they can't help how they behave. They will follow the dictates of their programming and instincts, not unlike animals. When that happens, you must forgive them "for they know not what they do" and forgive yourself as well.

When Christ Consciousness shines through the human, the human self doesn't become perfect, but it can become a vehicle for good, at least temporarily, rather than something that serves the ego and its drives and agenda. For Christ Consciousness to shine through you, your imperfections don't have to disappear; they simply need to be accepted. This doesn't mean indulging them, however. It means having compassion for them. By showering your imperfections with compassion, you become aligned with your divine self. Then those imperfections disappear for the time being.

Many imagine that being in the world but not of it means transcending the world and the ego and no longer being touched by the difficulties of the human condition. But that is not what this means. Rather, being in the world but not of it means that you fully embrace the world of form and embrace being human while knowing you are beyond all forms. To do this, you have to first love the world, including your humanness. You have to do the opposite of what the ego does, which is reject the world.

The ego rejects the world because it misperceives the world. When you stop seeing the world through the ego's eyes, you will love the world and know it as the magnificent creation and gift that it is. Then the perfection of your divine self can shine through your human self. You will be in the world but not of the world.

As long as you are in the world—as long as you are human—you will have some imperfections, issues, bad habits, and possibly addictions. These won't necessarily take you out of Presence unless you judge your human self for having them and think they shouldn't be there. Rejecting, judging, or going to war with your human shortcomings is what keeps you separate from your divine self. When you do those things, you are identified with the superego. Only the superego would go to war with the ego, because doing that accomplishes what the ego wants. It keeps people identified with the false self.

The remedy is to become aware of the interplay between these two aspects of your ego and to, instead, accept your human self. The instant you offer acceptance to your human self, you become your divine self, because the only thing that can do this is the divine self.

Sometimes you will fall short of your spiritual goals and ideals: You will not be loving, you will not be compassionate, you will not be patient, you will not be tolerant. You will gossip, lie, exaggerate, judge, blame, and get irritated. You will falter. But once you see that you've faltered and accept that, the slate is wiped clean. You are forgiven, and you can begin again.

Forgiveness is automatic as soon as you see that you have made a mistake. The seeing of the mistake *is* the forgiveness. Accepting that mistake will allow you to forgive yourself and move on. You are always forgiven, but if you don't forgive yourself, you'll stay stuck in the ego. Accepting that you made a mistake and that doing so is human allows you to forgive yourself. In that moment of forgiveness, you become a channel once again for Christ Consciousness.

If you have a negative tendency, such as judging or gossiping, do your best to not indulge in this. But if you do, acknowledge that you've made a mistake, accept that, have compassion for this human tendency, forgive yourself, and ask others for forgiveness if necessary. Then you will drop back into Presence, Christ Consciousness. To judge or berate yourself only keeps you separate from your divine self.

Before you can accept an imperfection, which stems from an imperfect thought, such as a judgment, you first have to become aware of that thought. That awareness is the beginning of dis-identification from the ego. That little step back achieved by witnessing thought is the beginning of realignment with the divine self.

This is exactly what is practiced in meditation: You become aware of a thought, you accept that it's there, and you forgive it and yourself for having it. Doing that allows you to return to Presence. This is the way from imperfection to perfection. There is no need to do away with imperfection; all that's needed is the right relationship to your imperfections. That relationship is one of acceptance, and that makes it possible to reunite with your divine perfection. The Divine is deeply in love with the human just as it is, because the Divine created the human to be just as it is.

Acceptance is the bridge that takes you from the human condition of suffering to the freedom and love of your divine nature. Without acceptance, you are stuck in the ego and the suffering it creates. With acceptance, the ego is allowed to be as it is, while recognizing that you are not that ego. You accept that you have an ego that causes suffering, but you also know that who you are, in essence, is divine. That mysterious essence is what sees the truth about the ego.

Then, after accepting and forgiving your humanness, there's one more very important thing to do: Don't go back to the thought-stream. Stay in Presence by staying in your body and senses and noticing the vast spaciousness from which you are looking, hearing, sensing, and experiencing. Notice it and sink into it. Remain in it. The only thing that can take you out of Presence is the voice in your head.

The longer you stay in Presence, the more this spacious sense of your divine self opens up, and you discover how very satisfying and complete it is. To be happy, you don't need what the ego thinks you need. The joy of pure existence is there whenever you turn the spotlight of your attention onto it and keep it there long enough for the divine self to open, like a flower, and release its fragrance.

The proof that you are not the ego, which is why you are able to accept the ego, is that you are *aware* of the ego. What is aware of the ego cannot be the ego. Just as the eye can't see itself, the ego can't see itself. Only something outside the ego can see the ego. You are able to be aware of what is going on within the human condition because you are not only human.

You are, in fact, what is aware of everything: thoughts, feelings, desires, intuitions, the sense of aliveness and existence, drives, urges, inspiration, and everything in the external world that is brought to you through the sense organ that is your body-mind. This awareness is perfect, unadulterated, and cannot be harmed by any imperfection. Nothing your human self has ever done has harmed the perfection of your divine self.

When you're in touch with this perfection and know yourself as this, you act accordingly, in peace, love, and kindness towards all. When this perfection infuses and is expressed through the human self, it is very beautiful indeed. But this doesn't do away with the ego, which will rise again and seek expression. Then awareness, acceptance, compassion, and forgiveness of the ego are called for again.

This is the dance between the human self and the divine self that continues moment to moment. Always, you—the one awakening from the egoic trance—must choose what you will express, who you will be, in that moment. Will you be the ego-dominated human self or the divine-infused human self? With practice, choosing the divine self becomes much easier, but that choice must still be made. That choice eventually becomes habitual, as ego identification was once habitual. But even then, the ego still exists in potential.

Being in touch with Perfection, or Presence, is also the secret to happiness. When you're in Presence, enjoying life is natural because you have no judgments or desires for life to be any different than it is. When you have no judgments or desires, your circumstances can't upset you. You just enjoy life as it is. You fall into the moment—you lose your egoic self—and that's enjoyable enough.

It's impossible to be ego-identified and be truly happy except briefly, because the ego is the manufacturer of discontentment, and by definition, you can't be happy when you're discontent. Unless you accept life just as it is, you can't enjoy it, because you're too busy resisting or trying to change it. When you stop having that kind of relationship with life, you drop into Presence and experience the natural in-joy-ment of the divine self.

The divine self is glorying in its creation—every aspect of it. It loves the puddles, the rainbows, the garbage, the feasts, the broken things, and the shiny and new things equally. To the divine self, there is no difference between these. They are all rejoiced in. To the divine self, everything is good, everything is the Beloved, all part of itself, its own creation.

If the ego felt this way about life, there would be nothing to desire, nothing to fear, and no better future moment to strive for. In other words, there would be little left of the ego, because you could say that desiring, fearing, striving, and looking to the future *are* the ego. If you were to cease doing these things, you would be in Presence, and the ego would lose its power and place. The ego would still be there in the background creating a sense of individuality so that you didn't fall into the Oneness and forget you were playing at being a human being. All the ego is really needed for is that.

The Duality Created by the Mind

Duality is not the truth but an illusion. Non-duality, or Oneness, is the truth. The duality of human and divine within every human being exists because the mind and ego create this duality, along with every other one. They create a sense of being separate from Oneness and a sense of separate things, even though the reality is Oneness. But this is not a mistake. Without this illusion, the experience of being a human being wouldn't be possible.

The mind—your brain—slices the world of form into pieces: things and concepts. This is useful and necessary for communication: When you want someone to pass the butter, it's helpful to have a word for butter and the concept of *pass*. However, things are not actually what you call them, and concepts are not actually real at all. Although language is a handy device, it's deceptive and contributes to misperceiving life.

Language doesn't represent reality very well. That isn't a problem if you don't expect it to. But to the mind, concepts and labels are real, so real that they replace reality with a virtual one, a mental reality. More importantly, concepts and labels cause the mind to overlook or dismiss the deeper reality. Concepts and language keep people on the surface of life, believing that life is as their minds tell them it is, when the truth is much more mysterious and unfathomable.

The ego doesn't like unfathomable. It prefers to know and doesn't like to not know. Knowing gives the ego the sense that it has some control. So it defines and labels, all in an attempt to know: "I know what that is. It's a tree." End of story. No need to look further. A tree is a tree.

But a tree is not just a tree, is it? Knowing the word for tree is not the same as knowing a tree. A tree, and everything else, is much more mysterious than the label it's given or anything you could say about it. What a complex and magnificent organism a tree is! How connected and interdependent it is with everything else! Without trees, there would be no human life on earth.

So is a tree really just a tree? How is it not equal to sentient life, itself, if sentient life is dependent on it? In a sense, then, a tree is part of the human body, not separate from it, since the human body is dependent on it. The same is true of the air and everything else human beings depend on for life. You aren't actually separate or independent at all from the rest of creation, and neither is anything else. Since everything is interdependent, you could say that everything is part of one body, one Whole, the Totality, the One.

But that's not all the mind does. It doesn't just label and classify and, in so doing, separate one thing from another. It does something else that creates further duality, further separation: It evaluates. It further separates things into good and bad, beautiful and ugly, young and old, fat and thin, short and tall, big and small, desirable and undesirable, and on and on. In other words, the egoic mind puts its own spin on things; it tells a story. Things are not just things. A thing or a person is thought to be whatever comes after the word for the thing or person: "That tree is...." "That person is...." "I am...." And that's a story.

Can a thing be defined in words? Can you be defined in words? Anything you say about something is bound to be inadequate and, as a result, essentially false, since so much is left out. Furthermore, is "is" or "am" *ever* true in this world of constantly changing forms, interdependency, and unfathomable complexity? Is anything that static and definable? This vainglorious attempt at definition is because the ego can't bear to not know. It has to say something about a thing or person. Then it can rest in feeling it knows that thing or person, even when it actually knows nothing more than it did.

This pretending to know is rampant in the egoic state of consciousness. When you look at your thought-stream, you see that it's full of half-truths, personal opinions, and attempts to know things that can't be known. How helpful can these thoughts be? Here are some examples:

He'll probably be late.

She's not very bright.

It won't take long.

It'll be great.

I can count on her.

I doubt he can do it.

I can't take it anymore.

She's not going to last much longer.

He's lazy.

I'm sure.

There's nothing wrong with these thoughts. They're the kinds of thoughts the egoic mind produces in everyone. It's just good to recognize that they aren't what they pretend to be—solid knowing and helpful truths. Meanwhile, life remains unpredictable. It is never the same, and neither are you nor anyone else. Who knows what you will do? Who knows what someone else will do? Who knows what someone is like? Who knows what the next moment will bring? You really don't know very much for certain. That's one thing you can be sure of.

When you drop into Presence, you know that you don't know, and that's fine with you. You even enjoy not knowing, just as you enjoy not knowing how a novel will end. Not knowing what's going to happen next makes life interesting and exciting.

The ego actually takes the fun out of life by pretending to know. Then it tries to put the fun back in by eating, drinking, shopping, and doing other things the ego likes to do, which bring only passing pleasure, not real happiness. The irony is that happiness is much more available than the ego realizes. It's just that you have to stop perceiving the world as the ego does and as language implies.

The egoic mind interferes with happiness by creating illusory dualities, such as good/bad, like/don't like, want/don't want, and better than/less than. The labels, themselves, often create the experience described. For instance, if you say, "I don't like vanilla ice cream," your ego is committed to not liking vanilla ice cream, or it will be proven wrong, which it likes even less than vanilla ice cream. As a result, your experience of vanilla ice cream will be influenced by the conviction that you don't like it. Because the ego is invested in upholding its opinions and beliefs, it will seek to have its experiences fulfill its expectations. In this way, the false self's beliefs often become self-fulfilling prophecies.

The ego likes dualities because it likes to take a stand, any stand. Taking a stand is what's important to the ego, not the particular stand, because taking a stand gives the ego an identity. Taking a stand is how identities are created: "I'm a Republican." "I'm against eating meat." "I don't like redheads." "I believe in getting up early." Taking a stand makes you feel like somebody, like an individual. And that is the definition of the ego, the false self: It is all the ideas that make you feel like a separate self, that make you feel special, all the ideas that masquerade as *you*.

There's nothing wrong with feeling like an individual. You are meant to be an individual in this world. In fact, you were given programming that makes you like certain things and not others, behave in certain ways and not others, and be driven to do certain things and not others. As part of your programming, you were given a personality with certain inclinations, drives, and preferences. Your personality is meant to influence your choices and behavior and to be a vehicle for your divine self, although it's more commonly a vehicle for the ego. It's just good to recognize that this programming isn't who you really are but, rather, a costume you've donned as you play the character you came to earth to play.

Personal preferences are only a problem when they're held so rigidly by the ego that they keep you from being in Presence. This happens if you aren't willing to be flexible about them, if you demand they be met when meeting them is not what's coming out of the flow. If, for instance, life is presenting you with vanilla ice cream instead of chocolate, it's best to say yes and enjoy it or "No thank you" and be happy with that too. To suffer over no chocolate ice cream would be to believe the thought "I don't like vanilla ice cream" or "They should have chocolate ice cream" or "They didn't care enough about me to have chocolate" or some other similar thought. The divine self goes with the flow: "What an adventure — vanilla ice cream for a change!"

Since the ego is very invested in and attached to its preferences, it wants them met. Not meeting them is a challenge to the ego's identity: "*I* don't eat vanilla ice cream!" The issue is not really the flavor of ice cream but a personal matter of identity, of who *I* am.

This is true of other dualities as well. The good/bad duality is equally a matter of identity for the ego. Because the ego generally feels that those who are similar to itself are good and those who are different are bad, knowing what *I* am like or not like is very important. That's how the ego determines how it relates to all the others out there. And, of course, everything deemed good is to be desired and acquired, while everything deemed bad is to be avoided.

This gives the ego a simple game plan. Keeping it simple is important to the ego, since it isn't one for complexity. Good/bad is about all it can handle. So the ego categorizes, and then it knows what to do: Go after good and avoid bad. The ego likes simple prescriptions, and dualities give it a simple prescription for living. The ego is a very primitive aspect of the human being. You don't really want it running your life. And yet, that is what's running most people's lives, because they're letting their thoughts guide them through life.

When something that's happening isn't judged as good or bad or as something you like or don't like, something very interesting happens: You lose your future! When you embrace whatever is, without judgment, there's no longer a need to look to a future for your happiness. You are already happy, and nothing needs to be added at some other point in time to be happy. When you're in Presence, there's no need for a future, which is just an idea anyway. The future is just the ego's fantasy about how it will finally be happy one day.

When you identify with the ego again, your future returns. The ego needs the future because the idea of a better future is how the ego justifies rejecting the present moment. The ego does this to keep you out of Presence and keep itself in charge.

Transcending Dualities

The key to transcending the egoic mind's dualities is recognizing them as dualities and learning to hold them lightly. As always, the first step is awareness: Be aware of the duality and untruth represented in your thoughts. Thoughts do not tell the truth. When you see this very clearly, your thoughts lose the power to make you suffer. As the children's nursery rhyme so wisely asserts: "Sticks and stones may break my bones, but words will never hurt me"—unless you believe those words. When you stop believing your thoughts, they stop hurting you, and you're less likely to hurt others with them.

To be aware of your thoughts, you first have to want to be aware of them. This may sound obvious, but your intention is important. You have to have that intention and then be curious enough about your thoughts to investigate them: What's going on there? Are they really the source of suffering? How do they do that?

The only thing that wants to be aware and can be aware and curious is the divine self. Yes, it is that close to you! It is what is curious, it is what's willing to look and willing to ask questions and discover the truth. It is all that is wise, good, and honorable in you and everyone else.

It takes no time to access the divine self because it's always here. It lives in the timeless dimension of Now, the only reality. The divine self is eternally present. If it weren't, you wouldn't be able to experience life, for although you appear to be a human, you aren't really a human being. Your human, or egoic, reactions to life are not your real reactions but your programmed reactions. You're programmed to behave like a human being, but you aren't one really (you just play one on TV). You are the curious, attentive, aware Presence that is experiencing life, including your human self. That's about all you can say about who you really are without getting into lies or distortions.

At a certain point in your evolution, this curiosity and willingness to question is activated. Then the false self begins to be deconstructed. Arriving at this point is Grace; you can't make it happen before its time. Fortunately, those who haven't reached this point aren't interested in making this happen, and those who'd like to be hit by Grace have already been. So here you are, and it's too late to turn back. The false self is doomed.

So let's take a look at some of the dualities that uphold the false self and its mental reality. One of the dualities that is most important to see through and transcend is the concept of better than/less than. Such comparisons play an important role in shoring up the ego. Like all dualities, this one is a lie and lends itself to a lot of stories and, consequently, a lot of suffering.

Better than or *less than* is always a point of view, a story. It is the point of view of the ego, whose agenda is to make you feel either inadequate or superior. If the ego can get you to believe in *better than* or *less than*, it will have succeeded in generating feelings of one kind or another. To the ego, the particular feeling isn't important. Feelings are important, however, because feelings are what make *better than* and *less than* seem true. Feelings give substance to the illusion spun by these words.

If, for example, you believe your mind when it tells you that you aren't as popular, good looking, intelligent, or spiritually advanced (all concepts) as so-and-so, you'll feel bad.

Feeling bad is proof that you've bought into that lie (but not proof of the lie). Your belief in the concept of less than and in the concepts of popular, good looking, intelligent, and spiritually advanced creates the experience of being less than someone else in these ways. So then you have that experience until your mind or someone else's tells you the opposite. Then you have that experience. In this way, people bounce back and forth between feeling bad about themselves and good about themselves.

The feelings generated by believing such thoughts put flesh on the false self, making it seem real. Who are you? "I'm less than.... I feel terrible." "I'm better than.... I feel good." Who is this "I"? It was created by thoughts. The false self is nothing but thoughts. If you stop believing your thoughts, you drop into the Silence of just being: the divine self. The ego is designed to keep you apart from the divine self, and it does this by telling stories that produce feelings.

Once you see this, such thoughts don't have as much sway. They still might affect you a little or for a little while, but not in the same way as before. Once you begin to see the truth about your thoughts, you keep seeing the truth. They can't fool you as they did before. You begin to see through more and more of the mind's lies. Little by little, the illusion is exposed, until it has big holes in it, which reveal the blue sky.

Dualities are transcended by recognizing the truth:

The duality of better than/less than is transcended by recognizing the truth that everything is perfect just as it is. Everything is as it's meant to be and serving its purpose in the Whole. You are exactly as you are meant to be in this moment, because you can't be any different than that. Given all the circumstances that created and led up to things being as they are, things can only be as they are, and that is perfect from the standpoint of the soul—perfect because it can be no other way. This is not perfection as the ego sees it. It is also not predestination, because although things can't be any way other than the way they are right now, they are also unpredictably becoming what they are. Nothing ever needs to change, and yet everything is constantly changing and evolving.

The duality of like/don't like is transcended by holding your preferences lightly, by noticing your preferences but not necessarily letting them drive your actions or decisions. Instead, the divine self determines your actions, which may sometimes take you in directions that go against your conditioned preferences and desires.

The duality of want/don't want is transcended by holding your desires lightly and by letting everything come that comes and letting everything go that goes. You lay the small will at the feet of Thy will, trusting that the divine self knows best and that "I want" and "I don't want" have little to do with what is naturally unfolding according to divine will.

The duality of good/bad is transcended by recognizing where those opinions come from and that they serve only the ego, and then holding them lightly or letting them go.

The duality of emotional highs and lows is transcended by coming into right relationship with life, which is experienced as equanimity. The integrated emotional state is one of being neither overly happy nor depressed, neither bored nor excited, neither hopeful nor despairing. Equanimity is the midpoint between the emotional highs and lows caused by believing your thoughts. This equanimity is sober, steady, okay with everything, at peace, and content. It is a state of causeless, subtle happiness, or inner joy.

The duality of taking too much (selfishness) or giving too much (not taking care of oneself) is transcended through selflessness. The "self" that is absent in "selflessness" is the egoic self, which tends to take or give too much, both for the purpose of getting what it wants. Selflessness, on the other hand, is giving appropriately, which is only possible when the egoic self is absent. In its absence, what's given is exactly what is needed in that moment and nothing more. The integration of this duality is the divine self moving in the world, doing or not doing, according to a greater will that knows exactly what action to take and when.

Creating Space

What happens when you become more aware of your thoughts and start questioning them is that space, or distance, is created between you and the thought-stream. Where once you automatically believed, gave voice to, and acted on your thoughts, now you notice them first, if only for a second. That second eventually lengthens, as you spend increasingly more time witnessing your thoughts, more time in the spacious Presence that is the divine self.

In the space that has opened up, there is now room to notice what's going on internally, where before there was no room, no space, to notice this. The bigger that space gets, the more room there is for questioning your thoughts. And the more your thoughts are questioned, the bigger that space becomes and the greater the distance between those thoughts and what's witnessing them. This distance eventually becomes so great that your thoughts seem like they don't belong to you. They're just one more thing arising in the field of consciousness.

With space, comes choice: You can choose to go back to thinking and believing your thoughts or not. Going back to your thoughts isn't as rewarding as it was before, though. You don't "enjoy" the egoic pleasure you once got from thought as much as you enjoy the equanimity of not entertaining thoughts. Sometimes you'll go back to your thoughts and sometimes you won't, but it will become increasingly apparent that you have a choice and that something is making that choice.

What is that? What can choose to go back into thought or stay in the spacious awareness of the divine self? This is where language fails. You could call it The Witness or The Chooser, but what is witnessing and choosing is not an object or a person like the things and people in the world of form. What you are is not an object that can be observed or quantified or understood. It can only be experienced.

What you are notices, experiences, chooses, moves, speaks, and does all the other things you think you are doing as a human being. But these things have never been done by a human being but, rather, by the force of life that you are, which operates *through* the human being.

You have always been this force, but you pretended to be human; and most of the time, you still pretend to be human. That's fine. Pretending is fine when you know you are pretending. It's only a problem when you don't know you're pretending. When the divine self is more integrated into the human being, you know yourself as divine while pretending to be human. Before that, the opposite was true: You thought you were the human being you were only pretending to be.

CHAPTER 3

Fully Human and Fully Divine

Being in Presence

Being in the world but not of the world is the experience of Presence. It is being fully human while also being fully divine. This is not a dry or detached place but an intimate, all-embracing, and in-love-with-the-world place. The experience is one of being fully involved in one's human life, while not being unduly influenced by the ego's perceptions or upset by the comings and goings in life.

To be able to embrace everything in the world, it's necessary to be "not of the world," meaning "not of the ego," which rejects the world because the world doesn't satisfy its expectations. Not being "of the ego" means not expecting the world of form to make you happy. Not having this expectation frees you from needing to have the world be a certain way. Then you can walk with lightness on the earth. You can be in the world, embrace it, and enjoy it fully just as it is, because your happiness is derived from something much deeper, from Presence.

Being in the world but not of it—being in Presence—is natural. Everyone knows what Presence is; everyone has experienced it. It is mysterious and yet most ordinary, because it's always here. It is the only thing that *is* always here. Everything else comes and goes within the spacious awareness that you are, which is Presence.

Does it seem strange to say that everything comes and goes in you? It's a radical idea, isn't it, that you are everything, that there is nothing other than you here? This is not the *you* that you think of yourself as, of course, but the *you* that everyone is, the Oneness that expresses itself in everything. This is the Oneness known by mystics. Oneness is the truth about life, but it is hidden by the forms of this life.

Oneness is often called the Formless to distinguish it from form. But form and the Formless are one and the same: Form is not separate from the Formless, which gives birth to form and expresses itself through form. Form and the Formless are intertwined and inseparable. Presence is the experience of the Formless, the timeless dimension in which you as a separate self do not exist. And yet, there is a form that claims to be you! You exist as both form and the Formless. This primary duality, which I've been calling the human self and the divine self, is at the core of who you are.

People seemingly get lost in form, in the human self, but that's never really possible. Like the clouds passing through the sky, thoughts can only temporarily block the truth about who you are. Sometimes you believe what your thoughts say about you, but there are many other times when you don't have thoughts or don't identify with them.

Once you have found your way to teachings such as this, you've undoubtedly had many glimpses of your true nature and likely some very profound experiences of it. The glimpses often come unexpectedly and in ordinary moments: when you're staring into the night sky, listening to beautiful music, gazing into your pet's or beloved's eyes, stepping outside on a spring morning, or looking up at the treetops or at a bird just outside the window.

What is it about these moments? Aren't they times when you are doing nothing else but looking, listening, and experiencing, when you are wide awake and attentive to what's being presented to you by your senses, and also when you're very much at ease? Being very alert and attentive to sensory reality and, at the same time, very relaxed puts you in contact with Presence. On the other hand, what people are usually attentive to—the thought-stream—produces anything but relaxation. You won't experience your divine self while thinking. But when your attention is completely engaged in the *experience* of your immediate environment, you feel alive and present.

There's a reason Presence is called that, and that's because it results from fully experiencing the present moment. You might argue that, since the present moment is all there is, it isn't possible to have any other experience than the present moment. But your mind takes you into an imaginary past and future, a virtual reality full of stories, like a movie. Being involved in this virtual reality means you're no longer fully in your body and senses. You are in the mind's reality, not the here and now. Because your mind takes you out of your body and senses, it takes you out of the present moment, out of Presence. The mind is the only thing that can do this. Without thought, you would always be in Presence. The fact that so few people spend much time in Presence is a testament to the power and allure of thoughts.

So if you want to know what Presence is, notice what the experience is like when you aren't lost in thought. People often touch so briefly into Presence that they think nothing of Presence. It seems like a nonexperience. But that's the mind's perception of Presence. People don't spend much time in Presence because their mind dismisses it as nothing and, therefore, useless. And so it is — useless to the ego.

Nothingness, no-thing-ness, has nothing to offer the ego. Presence is certainly not the kind of experience the mind is looking for. It isn't exciting or interesting enough for the mind, which loves drama, conflict, problems, and stories. You will definitely not find those in Presence, which is why the mind pulls you out of Presence every opportunity it gets.

The mind lures you out of Presence for another reason: Presence annihilates the false self, although only for as long as you are in Presence. This is definitely not an experience your mind wants to encourage! The same is true of meditation. Your mind resists it like the plague, because to the mind, meditation *is* the plague. And so it is.

No, the mind won't find anything of interest in Presence, nothing to complain about, nothing to analyze, nothing to compare or judge, nothing to think or talk about. The mind stops or goes silent or falls deeply in the background when you're in Presence because thoughts and Presence are incompatible. You can be absorbed in thoughts or in Presence but not in both.

In Presence, you might still have thoughts, but they aren't compelling, and you don't feel like *you* are thinking them or that they are yours, because in Presence, there is no *you*. Thoughts simply come and go in the background, if they're there at all, while sensory experiences take the foreground. Like the ever-shifting sounds, sights, smells, sensations, and other experiences available in any moment, thoughts become just one more thing arising and disappearing in awareness.

The result of being more fully in your body and senses is like seeing the world in Technicolor, when before it was only black and white. Living inside your head in a world of concepts and out of touch with your senses is very dead and deadening compared to the alternative. Concepts take the juice out of life, while being in the body and senses puts the juice back in. When you are more present, this becomes obvious. Life becomes richer, more beautiful, more vibrant, more alive, and more enjoyable. You've come Home, and something in you knows this.

Being present and in your senses is very pleasurable if you stay in that experience long enough. Usually people don't. They get a taste of Presence, and before that can deepen, their mind takes them into some mental landscape, where they lose contact with reality and their sensory experience. Until one develops the will or willingness to stay in Presence, that's the experience: You dip into Presence for a few seconds and then you're back in the mind.

To experience Presence more frequently and more fully, something within you has to want Presence more than the experience of thinking. The divine self awakening in you, or arising to awaken you, is what wants this. The will to be present can't be developed or forced but arrives in its own time. You either want to remain involved with your mind or you don't. This point is often reached when a person realizes that the thought-stream is the cause of suffering and he or she becomes motivated to get some relief from it. This point often coincides with a crisis or loss in someone's life.

This longing for Presence is a necessary ingredient, for without it, one's love affair with the mind is likely to keep winning out. However, this longing for Presence might continue for a very long time before someone becomes adept at staying in Presence. Many years or even decades of spiritual practice may be necessary before someone is able to stay in Presence for long periods of time. Nevertheless, every effort to do so is worthwhile and eventually pays off.

Moving into Presence

How do you move out of the ego into Presence? The obvious advice — don't get lost in the thought-stream — is only so helpful. Saying "Don't think" is a little like saying "Don't think of a pink elephant." Without replacing thinking with something else, you can't easily do away with thinking. What replaces thinking is sensory and body awareness.

The senses are doorways into Presence. When something like a sound, sensation, smell, taste, or stunning visual captures your attention, it stops your mind, if only briefly. You can't be fully engaged in your senses and in thought simultaneously. You are doing either one or the other. There is no alternative, nowhere else your attention can go. There is only the mind's virtual reality or reality, which is primarily a sensory experience.

As a result, becoming involved in your senses will bring you out of your head, into your body, and potentially into Presence. If a sensory stimulus is pleasant or striking enough, your attention naturally gravitates towards it and stays with it awhile. Getting lost in beautiful music or in a sunset doesn't take any effort or discipline because these experiences are inherently rewarding. In comparison to such pleasant experiences, the temptation to think is weak, until thinking overtakes them once again. Beautiful sights and sounds are what most commonly bring people into Presence when they stay with those experiences long enough.

Sensory experiences are also pleasurable simply because they provide a respite from the otherwise relentless mind. They take you away from something that is not so pleasant. People don't really want to think as much as they do. Thinking is more compulsive and habitual than actually rewarding. Anything that brings you more fully into your senses is not only pleasurable, but also a great relief from the usual state of consciousness.

Probably the most useful sense for becoming present is hearing, or listening, because even when sounds are absent, there is silence to listen to. The idea of listening to the silence in between sounds may sound silly, but listening to silence is a very special doorway into Presence. Because silence is usually ignored or goes unnoticed by the mind, giving your attention to it interrupts the mind's habitual way of listening and, consequently, takes you beyond the mind.

Listening to silence is powerful for another reason. Silence is a word that's often used to represent the Emptiness, or the Formless, from which form, including sound, arises. Just as forms emerge from the Formless, all sounds emerge from the Silence and then recede back into it. This is especially obvious in listening to a simple sound, such as the ringing of a bell. As you listen closely to a sound like that as it emerges from the silence and recedes back into the silence, your usual sense of self gets lost in the coming and going of that sound. The sense of *you* disappears with the sound into the Silence. And there you are in the Formless, as the Formless.

Furthermore, when you become familiar with the sound of Silence, or Emptiness, you will be able to tune into it even amidst noise. Silence, with a capital "s," is not only present in silence, but also in the midst of everything that is coming and going within the space of Silence. Listening to the Silence that permeates all of existence is, in fact, a very good meditation, centering device, or means of becoming more present.

This same experience can't be had through the sense of sight. Generally, something you see is either there or not there; it isn't seen emerging from or receding into the Emptiness. And sensations, tastes, and smells, although they emerge and recede, aren't nearly as distinct or available as sounds. So it is no surprise that sound—drumming, ringing gongs and chimes, chanting, and other kinds of singing and instruments—have been used throughout history to alter consciousness, or elicit Presence.

When you are in your senses, you are also in your body, which is a very different animal than the mind. Those who spend a lot of time thinking are often not in touch with what's going on in their body, including how their thoughts might be affecting their body. Thoughts have a tremendous impact on the body. They generate feelings, which are felt, processed, and often stored in the body. Stressful thoughts make the body tense, while calming thoughts relax the body. Furthermore, thoughts release chemicals in the brain, which regulate and affect the body in many different ways.

Your thoughts become the body's problem, which the body has to deal with in one way or another. So the best way to be good to your body is to move out of the thought-stream altogether. The only way to do that, however, is to be in your body and senses. For many, that means having to address some of the blocks and tightness caused by their thoughts and feelings. Consequently, many remain in their mind to avoid dealing with the body's pains and tension, which the mind created.

Still, there is no other route to Presence and therefore to true happiness and peace than through the body and senses. Getting into the body is a matter of giving the body your attention. This doesn't mean thinking about your body or imagining your body, but *experiencing* it by turning the spotlight of your attention on it. Your attention has to be on the body, not on thought.

Awareness and attention are the same thing, and you are this awareness, this attention. If there is a definition for who you really are, that's one of the best. It is one of the few things you can say about who you are that's close to the truth: You are what is aware. You are Awareness. You are attention to life. You are what is experiencing life through the mechanism of attention.

Whatever this attention lands on becomes lit up and amplified in your awareness. If it lands on your body, you become aware of the experience your body is having. If it lands on a thought, you become aware of that thought. If your attention remains there long enough, that thought will become your reality, as you identify with it. Or, instead, you might use your attention to investigate that thought. If your attention lands on a feeling, that feeling will be experienced and can be either identified with and thereby amplified or explored from Awareness.

If your attention lands on attention itself, a very interesting thing happens: You become aware of the Awareness that you are. However, since you are programmed to be identified with your body-mind, you usually won't stay identified with Awareness for long, unless you are self-realized. You will soon spring back into identification with thought, especially with the thought "I" and the body you imagine yourself to be.

Like a rubber band, your attention is drawn back again and again to the thought-stream and the false self, since that is your default programming. Eventually, the "rubber band" gets worn out and you stop identifying so readily, and you begin spending more and more time in Presence. At some point, your identity may permanently shift to Presence. That is called self-realization, or awakening.

A number of things can speed up this process of dis-identification from the false self, most importantly meditation and other spiritual practices. However, sometimes a trauma, a shock, or the loss of something crucial to one's identity causes the "rubber band" to weaken or break, and there is no returning to who you thought you were. This is an awakening of sorts, although possibly an unwelcomed one because the abruptness of this experience is so disorienting and confusing. If this experience is pathologized, as it often is, the person might return to ego identification but with a different identity, perhaps one of being someone who is mentally ill, unstable, troubled, or broken. And it is true that that person might need a lot of support in reestablishing a functional ego.

But for spiritual seekers who come to this point of awakening because they are ready to move beyond the false self, discovering that they *are* this Awareness or attention is very empowering, because then they can more consciously learn to direct it. If you're ready to be aware of Awareness and ready to direct your attention more consciously, then directing it to the sensations in your body and the experience of life coming in through your senses will take you more deeply into Presence.

The way to get out of your head and into your body is to turn your attention to what your body is experiencing, including what's coming in through your senses. At first, it might seem like nothing is going on, which is the mind's interpretation. It will say something like, "So what. What's the big deal? None of that's very interesting." You have to ignore the mind's disinterest and get very curious about what's going on in your body and senses anyway. If you hold your attention on the body and senses long enough, you'll discover that a lot is going on.

So you let the spotlight of your awareness notice whatever is coming in through your senses, including the sensations in your body, both subtle and not so subtle. The body is both physical and energetic, so these sensations may be either. Energetic sensations are experienced as energy flows or movements, aliveness, vibration, waves, tingles, or prickling or crawling sensations. The type of sensation is not important. What is important is that you notice your sensory experiences and your bodily or energetic sensations and allow them and experience them, without thinking about them or telling a story about them. Just notice everything that's happening in the here and now. If a thought arises, just notice that too, and then go back to sensing and experiencing.

When Awareness has fully drunk from one sensory experience, it will naturally move on to another and then another. The present moment is always changing, forever renewing itself. When you stay in Presence long enough, you'll notice this natural movement of Awareness from one sensory, energetic, or inner experience to the next.

Like a butterfly, Awareness lights on a sensation, then a thought, then an intuition, then a feeling. Then it sees something, then it hears something, then it imagines something. Then another thought arises, then a memory arises, and then a desire arises. Then Awareness lands on a sensation, a smell, a sound, a thought, and so on. This is the experience of continually living in Presence. Awareness experiences life, but it no longer identifies with any one thing for long, only enough to say yes to it and move on, as life naturally does.

This attention to what Awareness is naturally doing can also be a type of meditation. In meditation, with your eyes closed, notice what Awareness is aware of, as it moves from one sound or sensation to another, including more subtle energetic sensations. Let Awareness take you from one sensory experience to the next, as it will. Whenever a thought comes in or you catch yourself lost in thought, just notice that and gently return to sensing. Awareness follows the flow — it *is* the flow of life. The ego can interrupt this flow, bog it down, and cause it to get stuck, but the ego can never damage the flow, which remains untouched, unmarred, by any identification. Even that, the flow says yes to.

Residue from ego identification and the resulting emotions remains to some extent in everyone's body, in the energy field. This residue blocks the flow of subtle energy and the ability to experience the body and stay in it. One way to heal and release this residue is to slowly scan your body from head to toe with the spotlight of your attention. What you're looking for are any blank or dead spots in your energy field. These are areas of blockages, where the energy flow has gotten stuck due to unprocessed emotion.

As you scan the body, take as much time as you need to check in with each area: the top of the head, the forehead, the eyes, the ears, the nose, the cheeks, the mouth, the chin, the neck, the shoulders, and so on down to the toes. Is aliveness there? Stay in one spot until you can experience aliveness. Then move on to the next spot. The area you're focusing on should feel lit up, energized, vibrant. It might take some practice before you're able to experience this aliveness as strongly as is possible. Some people are able to experience this more easily than others, but with practice, anyone can feel the aliveness of the energetic body.

You'll see what I mean by vibrancy or aliveness if you focus on your hands, which is where most people can most easily feel this aliveness. When you let your attention rest on your hands for a few moments, you'll soon notice a subtle sensation of vibrancy, tingling, or energy. This aliveness runs throughout your body and can be experienced wherever you rest your attention, unless there is a blockage.

The spots where you have difficulty experiencing aliveness, which feel blank or dead, will need special attention, a special kind of awareness, one that is loving, patient, and allowing. When you gently hold your attention for a while on these areas, with curiosity and compassion, and allow them to be as they are, you'll notice a change in them. Aliveness may suddenly return, or you may sense a relaxation or a dropping into a deeper state, as something on a subtle level shifts. Sometimes when you're sitting with a block, information about it is received intuitively or as images.

What is most important for you to understand is that your attention, curiosity, acceptance, love, and compassion are enough to release and heal a block. This healing happens on a mysterious level. Often no understanding of what is happening is even needed. And yet, sometimes further understanding is received. Doing a body scan like this daily or weekly is a very good practice, one that will help keep your body's energy flowing and keep you in good health.

Staying in Presence

What makes staying in Presence more likely is the developing awareness that, in any moment, you are consciously or unconsciously choosing to stay there or not. Awareness that you have a choice and awareness of what you are choosing develops, until staying in Presence becomes a choice-less choice, one you no longer have to consciously make because you've made it so many times before.

One trick to staying in Presence is to not go to war with your thoughts. How you relate to thought from Presence is important, or you'll get pulled back in. If you consider the thoughts in the thought-stream to be bad or problematic, that will only activate the ego and mind further, as the false self gets busy trying to solve that so-called problem.

The way to relate to thoughts is with kindness and as you would a child who doesn't know any better. After all, the egoic mind is a primitive, outmoded aspect of the mind and can't help being the way it is. As with a child, you accept that the child is ignorant, and you don't expect the child — the mind — to be any different. But you also don't give your attention to the mind's childish ways. That only strengthens it. Like a parent, the spacious awareness that you are is nonreactive, compassionate, kind, wise and patient towards thoughts.

The best approach to the mind is to let it be as it is, without demanding that it change in any way. Just let your thoughts be as they are and leave them alone. Eventually, you'll lose interest in them, just as you would with anyone who lies, complains, throws tantrums, bores you, or is unpleasant in other ways. The more you are able to leave your thoughts alone, the more they will subside and the less troublesome they will be.

To stay in Presence, you also have to become as interested in Presence as you were in your thoughts. This curiosity has to be cultivated, as it isn't as automatic as people's fascination with thought. What is Presence like now? And now? Give your full attention to Presence and allow yourself to sink into it. How do you sink into Presence? You have to be willing to explore this for yourself. Are you willing to do that? If not, what keeps you from doing that? What argument does the ego come up with?

The key to sinking more deeply into Presence is to keep noticing. This noticing is like listening, but with your whole being, not just your ears. This noticing is more like a way of being—of being open, receptive, attentive, curious, and expectant, while remaining very much here, now. It is as if you're listening for something in the distance or expecting something to arrive soon, as if something very important is happening or about to. You give the moment your full attention, as if it's the only thing happening in the world—and it is! It's the only thing that's real in your immediate world.

Presence is also called Stillness, and for a very good reason: Stillness is one of its qualities. So when you become very still and imitate stillness or focus on this quality, you drop more deeply into Presence. This is why most meditation is carried out in stillness and silence. These are qualities of Presence. Again, this is something you have to explore for yourself, as reading about Stillness is not the same as experiencing or exploring it. Are you willing to explore Stillness for yourself? If not, how does your mind keep you from doing that?

Another quality of Presence is peace. Can you find it within you, this very subtle peace? Look for it, and when you catch a glimpse of it, focus on it. Then the experience of peace will grow. This is true of every quality of Presence: Focusing on that quality brings that quality, and Presence, more strongly into your awareness.

If you are experiencing any of the qualities of Presence — peace, love, compassion, clarity, fortitude, joy, gratitude — give that quality your attention; become curious about it. What is that like? Stay with that experience and see what you can discover. Doing this will take you more deeply into Presence, as that quality opens up more fully to you. This often happens naturally in meditation, but you can do this as an exploration anytime.

This explains why positive thoughts, affirmations, and expressions of love and gratitude bring you into Presence. By imitating the experience of being in Presence, they evoke Presence and act as a bridge into it, where you naturally feel positive, loving, grateful, at peace, and in awe of life.

Awe is another quality that, when evoked and focused on, can take you into Presence or more deeply into it. Young children are naturally in awe of this world, as their perceptions haven't been deadened yet by names and concepts. When children see a flower, for instance, it's as if they're seeing it for the first time, without any ideas about it, which may actually be the case.

Awe is evoked by looking at something, as young children do, without any labels or concepts. This is something you can practice doing. When you are looking at something, just notice the judgments and concepts that come to mind, such as *beautiful, old, messy, small,* or *dirty.* Then let those labels drop away, as they naturally will if you don't agree or disagree with them. Your thoughts want your agreement, or even your disagreement, because once you take a stand, you've joined the ego's world. Then more thoughts rush in to support that stand.

Being in Presence is a place of neutrality and equanimity, where everything is accepted and equally loved. Presence doesn't take a stand, unless you consider that love is a stand. When everything is held equally, there is no stand but love. This is why Presence is so peaceful. Life isn't chopped up into good or bad, like or don't like. Everything is embraced, which brings peace. Without language separating one thing from another, there is no comparing, analyzing, judging, or sizing up, no pushing away or grasping. There's no need to think at all.

This brings us to a very important point: Presence operates from a larger intelligence than thought. If you stay in Presence long enough, you'll get to know this Intelligence, which is you and which has the whole universe within itself. If you stay in your mind, however, recognizing that another intelligence is at work in your life will be more difficult, because you'll be busy marching to the drumbeat of your thoughts. You can only have one master. Fortunately, everyone has moments when they respond to the deeper intelligence within, which doesn't use thoughts to communicate. To understand what it would have you do, you have to be present and notice how and where it is moving you in the moment.

Acting and Speaking from Presence

Everyone knows what it's like to act and speak from Presence, and everyone knows what it's like when others are acting and speaking from Presence. There's a distinct quality about it that makes everyone relax and feel good. The experience is one of lightness, playfulness, harmony, joy, peace, love, ease, and openness. Presence is open to others and open to life, in love with others and in love with life, and at peace with others and at peace with life. Presence is how everyone wants to feel all the time. And yet, it is relatively rare for most people.

Speaking from Presence is an experience of unpremeditated expression: Something comes to be said, and you open your mouth and say it without knowing what that will be. Here are some other signs that speaking is coming from Presence:

❖ It feels good to say whatever you're saying, and others feel good hearing it.

❖ There is a sense of rightness about what you are saying that is different from the certainty of the ego. This rightness has a feeling of wonder and expansion, unlike the ego's certainty.

❖ You have a sense that what you are saying is coming from beyond yourself.

❖ You feel you have touched into something deep or profound.

❖ You feel goosebumps.

❖ You feel surprised at the wisdom of what you just said.

❖ You say something you've never thought of before.

❖ You and others feel uplifted and inspired.

Speaking from Presence is very different than egoic speech. When the ego wants to express something, it formulates its thoughts first, often in the midst of supposedly listening to someone else. Then, the first chance it gets, it inserts those remarks into the conversation. Or it might blurt something out without having thought it through first. When that happens, the communication tends to be full of emotion and ego, and it tends to activate other people's emotions and ego.

Speaking from Presence, on the other hand, isn't likely to activate other people's emotions and ego. Rather, it tends to bring others into Presence, along with you, although there are exceptions to this. Some egos are determined to try to bring you down to their level and not give in to Presence. If this is happening, you can't do much about it except have empathy for those caught so deeply in ego and in their own self-induced suffering. There's no point going to battle with other people's egos any more than with your own. The best approach is meeting other people's egos with compassion while not feeding their ego or yours in any way.

Acting from Presence is very much the same as speaking from Presence: You find yourself doing something without having decided to do it and without questioning why you are doing it just then. This might sound like or even appear to be conditioned action, but unlike the ego, when Presence moves you, there is no resistance, only ease. Furthermore, from Presence, what you do is unaccompanied by thoughts. There is no strategizing, planning, rehearsing, or weighing of pros and cons, nor are there any evaluations, judgments, or thoughts about the past or future. You're in the moment and doing what you're doing because that is what is arising in you to do. And you're doing it, not to achieve some goal, but because doing it is, itself, rewarding.

In Presence, you move spontaneously, fluidly, easefully, and without thought. Doing just happens. Maybe you suddenly pick up the phone to call someone, or find yourself taking a different route home, or end up browsing through books in a bookstore, all of which lead to information or opportunities you needed but didn't know you needed. Presence's way is both mysterious and ordinary. Its guidance is hidden amidst the mundane activities of your lives.

Something very profound is behind life and guiding your life, although it often doesn't seem that way, and you won't convince the ego of this. The ego feels alone in a desperate and unsafe world, so you won't get any confirmation or understanding from the ego about this mysterious dimension of life. The ego knows nothing about it. And yet, many do know this dimension with something other than their minds. That knowing is neither blind faith nor belief, but something that feels very solid, very true.

Overcoming Challenges to Being Present in the World

Being in Presence is not so difficult when you're sitting quietly in a beautiful setting or meditating, but how do you stay in Presence in this busy, stressful world full of egos and in the midst of taking care of your responsibilities?

Once you start moving or doing something, the mind comes online in a way that it was not when you were still. While a still body helps keep you in touch with Presence, doing does the opposite: It activates the mind. Suddenly, the drill sergeant in your head steps forward and gives you your marching orders: "Do this now, and hurry up!" If you respond to such orders, or even to more gentle suggestions or seemingly helpful advice, you are in the ego's world. It's got you until you do one thing: Notice that you're doing the ego's bidding. This is often pretty obvious. When you are, you're usually hurrying, stressed out, worried, or in some other way discontent.

Once you notice you're identified with the ego, however, you are no longer identified! Noticing *is* Presence. The only thing that can notice identification or anything else is Presence. Then it's up to you what you do with that awareness. You might go right back into identification or, instead, use that awareness to choose to turn away from the thought-stream.

Doing comes from one of two places: from the ego in response to a thought or mental directive, or out of the flow as a spontaneous urge to act. This flow is Presence, and it is alive and intelligent. The flow is constantly moving, and it moves you according to a greater will. When you are present, right action and speech flow out of the moment. This greater will also allows you to follow the ego's will and to not be in the flow. The Intelligence behind life is very benevolent and lets you identify with the ego and have that experience, or be in Presence and have that experience. These will be two very different experiences, however, and will feel very different.

When you're in the flow, or in Presence, you feel relaxed, at ease, without problems, and content. This is because the false self has dropped away. In Presence, the self you imagine yourself to be gets lost or swept up in the doing, and that can't help but be enjoyable.

When you are ego identified, you feel the opposite. You're not immersed in or enjoying what you're doing but hurrying and absorbed in thoughts about what else needs to be done or about something else. The ego is like having a parent looking over your shoulder, telling you what to do and evaluating your every move. It's no wonder people find themselves rushing to the next activity when the current one is so unpleasant. The ego is always hurrying to another, hopefully better, moment. But if you bring the ego into that new moment too, you'll be just as unhappy.

So why does anyone listen to the ego? The answer is, you can't help it because listening to that voice is the default of the programming you've been given. The ego belongs to your human nature. Until you realize your divine nature, you have little choice but to follow your programming. Once you realize there is a choice, however, everything changes. You are at that point now. You've realized you have a choice. Still, you have to learn new ways of doing things. The drill sergeant needs to be quieted and a new voice heard.

This new voice, the one that guides your activities, doesn't actually have a voice like the old master, the ego. In fact, it is silent, and it is found in silence, by both being silent mentally and by being in Silence and then listening. To hear this new master, you have to be receptive, still, and attentive rather than thinking.

When you become aware that you're marching to the ego, there are several things you can do to shift to a new, kinder master:

1. **Stop whatever you are doing.** This breaks the egoic trance and allows for new possibilities. You might also include snapping your fingers, tapping your thigh, blinking your eyes, smiling, or engaging in some other physical cue that signals this break with the egoic mind and anchors you in your body.

2. **Take at least one deep breath.** More is better. This calms the sympathetic nervous system, which may have been activated by stressful thoughts.

3. **Notice your surroundings, your breathing, and your hands.** What are you seeing and hearing? Look around,

listen, notice your breathing, and look at your hands. Sometimes just looking at your hands is enough to ground you in your body. Even taking just a minute to do these things will begin to shift your state.

4. **Notice your body.** Notice how it feels to be in your body. Don't be concerned if you feel stressed, tense, anxious, or uncomfortable in any other way. Just notice this and let it be. If your mind comments on how you feel, just notice that thought and any other thoughts, let them be there, and return to noticing your bodily sensations and letting everything be as it is. You don't need your mind to tell you how you feel, since your Intelligence already knows. Your animal body is telling you something. Just listen to it a moment. Like a kind parent, give it your compassionate attention, and it will begin to relax all by itself, just by giving it loving attention.

5. **Notice what is noticing.** Notice what is aware of the body, the sensations, and your surroundings. Notice the quiet, unobtrusive stillness of Awareness. Notice how it notices and accepts everything. It is like the still eye of a hurricane, motionless and silent in the midst of whatever is happening.

6. **Notice the experience of Presence.** Is there aliveness? Is there peace? Let yourself sink into the aliveness, peace, relaxation, gratitude, awe, or any other quality of Presence that might be there. That experience is the truth, that is reality, and that is what's important. Nothing in the world of form is as important as Presence, and everything that is truly meaningful and fulfilling comes from Presence.

7. **From Presence, find out what is true.** Is it true to continue what you're doing, do something else, or do nothing? How does Presence want to move? How is it moving you or not moving you now? What is true, here and now, in this moment? Check within, because you do know, but you have to pay attention to the more subtle realm of Presence.

Once you are grounded in Presence and begin doing something again, take it slower and keep checking in with Presence. Try to stay connected with that still point within. If you move too quickly, Presence tends to get lost. Moving more slowly is key because this thwarts the ego's tendency to hurry and allows Presence to enter into whatever you are doing.

Move slowly enough to stay in your body and senses, and notice your body's experience. For instance, notice and experience your arm as it reaches for a cup, your foot as it touches the ground, your fingers as they type, your hands as they wash a dish, your whole body as it bends to pick up something. Notice the sounds and smells in your environment. Take in whatever you're looking at as if for the first time. Be the space in which all this doing is happening.

Don't forget to also notice the aliveness and any other qualities of Presence that might be showing up: the gratitude, peace, love, subtle joy, and contentment of your divine self. Notice, also, any wisdom, insights, inspiration, or knowings that might be bubbling up. All of this will be missed if you are hurrying and listening to the mind.

Also, pause and take a breath regularly to make sure you're still connected to Presence. Pausing gives you an opportunity to tune in and "listen" to Presence and ask: "Am I still in the flow? Where is the flow going now? What is it moving me to do now?" Without pausing and tuning in regularly, the egoic mind can easily co-opt Presence. You'll know when that happens by how you feel.

Once you begin living more from Presence, you learn to trust that the divine self knows how to move you in ways that are not only satisfying, enjoyable, creative, and wise, but also productive and safe. Your divine self is very practical and knows how to support your safety and survival, not only your happiness. The divine self has been waiting all your life to take over and live you. You only have to step out of the way and trust that it will do that beautifully. That means putting your mind aside long enough to discover what is arising to say or do, or not do, in any moment.

No matter how well seated you are in Presence, however, the level of ego in others and in the world, in business, in schools, and in other institutions and organizations, makes staying in Presence challenging. If you didn't have an ego yourself, the level of ego in the world would be far less challenging. But egos activate other egos, and that's the problem. The problem with being in the world, then, is a problem within you and not really with the world. And that is important to see. The world doesn't have to change a bit for you to be in Presence, and from Presence, for you to have an impact on the world. You just have to learn to hold your own in the world.

One thing that helps is simply knowing that egos activate your own ego and that other people's egos will try to pull you into their state of consciousness. Egos can't help doing this. But you can help yourself stay in Presence by remaining conscious and aware while speaking and interacting with others.

Here are some of the things egos do to draw you into their world:

❖ **Egos state an opinion to elicit an opinion** from you, and then the debate is on! Egos love debating because they love demonstrating that they're right or smarter than someone else, although their opinions rarely prove that. Egos need to be right, and for that, an opinion is needed. Opinions are also good for stirring up emotions and creating drama, which egos also love. The problem with opinions is that none of them contains the whole truth.

❖ **Egos tell stories** about what happened to them because those stories and the emotions they stir up give them a sense of identity: "This happened to *me.*" By retelling those stories, they get to keep their self-images, which the false self needs to exist. This same enjoyment of stirring up emotions can be seen in the news media.

❖ **Egos complain.** Sharing likes and dislikes is a favorite pastime of egos: "I like this," says one. "Oh, I don't like that," says another. This passes as comradery, but what it really does is shore up the sense of "I." Now you have taken a stand. Now you are somebody.

❖ **Egos judge others**. Egos love to talk about others, often under the guise of sharing information and insights or trying to understand or fix other people. However, within such conversations is generally an agenda on the part of the egos to prove themselves right and superior to others.

❖ **Egos love to give unsolicited advice.** While pretending to be helpful, advice is often a type of opinion and serves to position the one giving the advice as right or superior. Although wisdom coming from Presence might appear at times to be advice, usually those receiving such wisdom can tell the difference between that and the ego's advice, and they respond accordingly.

These types of communications are red flags pointing to the ego. From Presence, there is only clear seeing of this, compassion for the human condition, and acceptance for this being the way it is. Any judgment you have around these things is just more ego to be noticed and have compassion for. Others are the way they are, and in that moment, they can be no other way than that. The same goes for you as well.

The best approach for dealing with egoic communications is to listen quietly without chiming in with your own opinions, judgments, advice, stories, or complaints. This will keep you from getting pulled into the thought-stream that's coming out of other people's mouths. Just notice what's being spoken without identifying with it, without agreeing or disagreeing with it. When you're noticing from a place of neutrality, equanimity, and compassion, you know you are in Presence.

The funny thing is, the less you say in most conversations, the nicer you're likely to seem to others and the nicer you're likely to actually be. The impulsive need to speak is almost always the ego, as it pushes forward to get some need met by the conversation: to be right, to be seen as smart, or to gain approval. Curtailing that impulse to speak keeps the ego out of the conversation and gives Presence a chance instead.

By being quiet, you are making space for Presence in the conversation, and people will feel that. Then speak only when you're moved to speak by Presence. Just as you might wait before answering an email, waiting a moment before speaking will help you stay connected to Presence and make it more likely you'll express Presence instead of the ego when you do speak.

Here are some tips for staying in Presence when you are having a conversation:

❖ Notice what others are saying and where it is coming from — the ego or Presence.

❖ Notice what your own thought-stream might be producing in response to theirs.

❖ Keep your attention on what you're experiencing in the here and now, on the aliveness in your body and on your sensory experience.

❖ Stay seated in what is noticing. Stay with *what* is aware.

❖ When you're speaking, be attentive to how much ego is in what you are saying, particularly in your "I" statements.

When you say "I," notice what that's like. Can you hear the ego? Can you feel it? Your own Presence is what's able to know this. Being identified with the ego feels tight, contracted, and icky. The more identified you are with "I," the less good you feel about yourself and the stronger the need is to defend yourself, be right, and be special.

Those who have very little identification with the ego have difficulty even saying "I" because that seems so false. So if you have a hard time saying or believing "I" or believing what you're saying after you say "I," that's a very good sign. It means you aren't very identified with the false self. Noticing that you believe what you're saying to different degrees, even as the words are coming out of your mouth, is an excellent practice. Eventually you'll be left mostly with words that come from Presence.

The degree to which you believe what you're saying is the degree to which you are identified with the false self and also the degree to which Presence is there, since Presence is what notices identification. The more ego, or identification with thought, there is, the less Presence there is; the less ego, or identification with thought, there is, the more Presence there is.

The word identification gives the impression that ego identification is either happening or not: You are either identified or not. But rather than being black or white, there are many shades of identification, just as there are many degrees in which you believe something. You may believe, or be identified with, a thought just a little or completely. Those are two very different experiences of thought and two very different states of consciousness. The egoic state is one in which you believe your thoughts without question. The enlightened state is when you no longer believe your thoughts.

Talking about yourself can be a slippery slope: You may start out not identified at all with "I" and end up more identified than you'd like. Limiting how much you say at any one time will make it less likely that your ego will step in and take over. Both conscious and unconscious people often start out speaking in equanimity and aligned with love and good intentions, but then the ego slips in and inserts its point of view, and the emotions—the clouds—begin to roll in. State what you want to say briefly, and then stop and let others speak. Find out what they have to bring to the flow of conversation.

Being present to others stands a chance of bringing others into Presence with you. Presence is not only good for you, but for everyone. So although egos can activate your ego and get it going in directions you don't want to go, being in Presence can activate Presence in others and help turn the world around, one person at a time.

From this chapter, it would be impossible not to conclude that your conversations and interactions with others will change dramatically once you begin living more from Presence. One of the ways they're likely to change is that you'll lose interest in being with those who are deeply invested in their egos and uncomfortable or unfamiliar with Presence. Your friends just might change, but that's okay. Other people will take their place, or you'll simply enjoy more time alone or with your loved ones.

CHAPTER 4

Clearing the Clouds

Dis-identifying with Thought

To return to our earlier cloud analogy, clearing the clouds doesn't necessarily require that the thoughts in the thought-stream be cleared away. Thoughts can and may remain in the thought-stream without causing significant obstruction to Presence as long as they aren't strongly identified with. The degree of identification with thought is what's key, not so much the number of thoughts.

Nevertheless, the number of thoughts in the thought-stream diminishes as belief in them does. The less attention given to a thought, the less it is fed. Eventually it weakens and stops arising altogether. Then the process of clearing accelerates, since the fewer thoughts there are, the easier it is to dis-identify with them because more Presence is available to see through them. Once a lot of Presence is available, it would take either a barrage of thoughts or an upsurge of feelings to squeeze out Presence.

Identification is a measure of how much you believe a thought. For instance, if you had the thought "I want a pink elephant," you probably wouldn't identify with it because it's so unbelievable. The reason thoughts like that don't generally arise in the first place is because they wouldn't be believed. The thoughts in your thought-stream are ones you believe to some extent, or they wouldn't arise.

Identification is a process of taking on certain beliefs as your own, as belonging to the imaginary *you*. These beliefs, in turn, create and maintain this false, imaginary self. Your particular beliefs produce feelings, desires, and drives, which result in actions that shape and maintain a particular identity. The more strongly you believe a thought or desire, the more power it has to shape your life.

The problem with your thoughts, beliefs, and egoic desires is that the false self they create is a self that suffers. To disidentify with your thoughts and stop suffering, the truth about your thoughts has to be seen. Once you see how they cause suffering and only pretend to be useful, you can begin to let go of them. When it comes to thoughts, seeing is *not* believing. In other words, seeing the truth about your thoughts leads to not believing them.

Let's take a look at how the thought "I" causes suffering, since this is the core thought. All suffering starts with belief in "I." The "I," or false self, is the only thing that has desires, preferences, dreams, and fears. (It's funny how a thought can have thoughts!) Presence, your true self, has none of these. Its only "desire" is to experience life fully, to drink it in, all of it, even what the false self refuses to embrace.

So "I" is the generator of suffering. Desires, fears, preferences, and all other manner of thoughts set this "I" up against the world, against life. Without this resistance to life, to however life happens to be showing up, there would be just life, just this, and just this would be okay. Even saying that, is inaccurate, since "okay" is a judgment. Such is the problem with language. Because it's dualistic, it contributes to the very push-pull that defines the "I" and how it experiences the world.

To be more precise, "I" isn't actually the problem. When "I" stands alone and merely points to the fact that you exist and are conscious and aware, that is the true "I." The trouble starts with the definitions that come after "I," which turn "I" into the false self: "I'm alone. I'll never make it. I'm going to fail at this. I don't know what to do. I give up." These are the stories that create the imaginary self that you think of as yourself. Without these thoughts, you'd simply be "I."

If all the "I" thoughts were cleared out of the thought-stream or not believed, you would be enlightened because you'd experience yourself simply as "I" or "I am," without any definition to it, just pure existence. And that's the truth. That's what you are: pure existence, without a beginning or an end, playing at being a self with a history, desires, fears, preferences, and dreams. You are existence having a human experience.

But, of course, those "I" thoughts probably won't disappear, and you'll still need to use "I" in speaking with others. What changes with enlightenment is that you know you're not what those thoughts describe, so you're able to hold those thoughts lightly. You don't really believe what the "I" thoughts say about you. You know they only describe the false self.

This lightness towards yourself, towards the self described by your thoughts, means you have more choice around those thoughts. You can act on them or not. You can choose which ones will shape your life and which ones won't. That character has to do something—it has to have a life. So naturally, it will live out some of those desires and identify with some of those thoughts to some extent.

On the other hand, if you assume your thoughts describe who you are and what you need to do, you have little choice. You'll be whatever your thoughts say you are and do whatever your thoughts tell you to. You won't feel you have a choice to pick and choose which thoughts to follow. Then, like most people, you'll be tossed to and fro by whatever thought happens to pop into your mind.

People are at the mercy of their programming usually until it causes them so much suffering that they stop and take a look at what's going on. Suffering wakes people up out of the programming. That is Grace. Suffering is the divine self sending a message: "Look at what your thoughts are doing to you and to others!" As the suffering breaks *you* (the false self), a break in the clouds appears where the sun shines through. Then the laser-like clarity of the sun begins to dissipate the clouds, one by one, as it cuts through the lies, misunderstandings, and deception of the thoughts in the thought-stream.

How to Stop Believing Your Thoughts

What makes not believing something possible is seeing that it isn't worth believing. If a belief or other thought is beneficial, then it's worth keeping. However, once you begin examining your thoughts more closely, you won't find many worth keeping. You'll discover that your beliefs and other thoughts are of very limited or no value and often quite detrimental, as so many are untrue.

The funny thing about thoughts is they seem so true, even when they aren't. How can that be? And why would that be? The answer is, your thoughts are programmed to be believable for the purpose of creating an illusory self. This self couldn't exist if you didn't find your thoughts irresistible and believable.

The illusory self is the thought-based, mind-created self. It is just images of you, the *you* that you imagine yourself to be and the *you* that the voice in your head seems to be. This illusory self is what I've been calling the false self, and for a good reason: It's an imposter self. It is part of your programming, but not the entirety of it by any means. At a certain point in your evolution, you start seeing through the false self, and it begins to dissolve and loosen its hold. Before then, however, the false self serves evolution by creating suffering and delivering certain lessons.

To be in the world, the divine self needs a costume. It needs a body-mind, a personality, drives, talents, tendencies, preferences, and some ego in order to play a role in the world and to function. All this is accomplished through programming. You might be surprised to discover, however, that you don't need thoughts about yourself—your "I" thoughts—to be somebody or to be a functional human being. The thoughts in your thought-stream actually interfere with you being the best human being you can be. Those thoughts only *seem* to be helpful and *seem* to be true and *seem* to be you.

You don't need the false, mind-generated self. That programming is destined to go eventually, which is what the process of enlightenment is all about. The false self eventually dissolves to the extent that you stop identifying with your thoughts, while the character you're playing retains a personality with preferences, drives, inclinations, talents, some ego, and other essential programming or conditioning.

You are here to experience being a human, to learn and grow, and to play a role in the drama on earth at this time. Until now, the thoughts in your thought-stream have been integral to this experience. The voice in your head has served your personal evolution as it was meant to. This voice has been responsible for the suffering that's been the grist for the mill of your evolution, and it's brought you to this teaching. However, it's likely that now, for you and for many, the voice in your head is no longer serving your evolution, because you are ready for the divine self to incarnate more fully. Two thousand years ago, I came to demonstrate that divine incarnation was possible, as have many others before and since. And now it may be your turn. For many of you, this is possible within this lifetime.

You are meant to be both human and divine. The drives, desires, dreams, fears, beliefs, and other thoughts in the thought-stream provide lessons and some design and impetus for your human life. They give you an identity, something to do, and challenges to evolve and strengthen you. However, at some point, it's time for the thoughts in the thought-stream to be shed, for the clouds to be cleared, and the human self to live more purely, without those thoughts and the delusion and suffering they cause. It's time for the caterpillar to turn into a butterfly. This transformation results in a kinder, more compassionate and happier human being. But you'll still be human, with the same personality and many of the same quirks, tendencies, preferences, drives, and even some of the same psychological issues.

The programming that belongs to the costume serves a purpose and isn't meant to completely go away. However, once you realize your true nature, your relationship to that programming changes. You wear your costume more lightly, never forgetting your true identity, and follow your programming only when it's true to do so. Something wiser than the programming steps in and takes the programming's place much of the time. What is capable of discriminating how and when to apply the programming and how to move in the world is the divine self—the Heart—which is something that will be explored later. For now, let's return to how to become free of thoughts that don't serve you.

If you believe a thought is serving you, you'll consciously or unconsciously reinforce it and have trouble dis-identifying with it. However, once you stop believing a thought, it's only a matter of time before it drops away. Thoughts you don't believe won't remain in your mind. So assume that the thoughts in your mind are ones you still believe and also assume they probably don't deserve to be believed.

Become the skeptic when it comes to your thoughts. Stop trusting them. For that, you have to be committed to noticing your thoughts and willing to question them until you're thoroughly convinced that the entire thought-stream has little value. You have to discover this about the thought-stream for yourself through your own investigation.

As you witness your thoughts, some of them will instantly be seen to be untrue. Those are the ones you don't believe very much, and they won't require further investigation. They'll eventually stop arising if you continue to just notice them — "There you are again, my friend" — and then turn your attention to something in the here and now.

As you do this witnessing, try to be aware of any subtle or not so subtle judgment you may have about your thoughts, because that's a form of attention. If the attention you give a thought is "Hey there, see you later," that's fine because that's an expression of witnessing and allowing. That kind of relationship to a thought releases it instead of perpetuating it. However, if you feel any upset, judgment, or irritation about a thought, that signals the unconscious to keep sending that thought. This might sound insane, but there is some insanity in all of this.

For thoughts you believe more strongly, brushing them off won't be as easy. One example might be "I'm getting fat." This thought may appear to be an objective statement of fact, but it's really a disguised judgment that pretends to be helpful. It's easy to assume you need that thought or surely you will get fat. But is that true? The falseness of such thoughts is not so obvious, nor is the ego's hidden agenda.

That thought, like so many others, has a big emotional hook in it and is likely to be connected to many other thoughts you also believe. This thought will probably require thorough investigation along with any other thoughts and emotions related to it. Writing down all the thoughts connected to it can be very helpful. Examples of related thoughts might be: "I should weigh less. I should look different than I do. Having fat is bad. Being fat is terrible. Fat is ugly. Being fat means I'm a failure. Being fat is going to ruin my life. No one will love me. I'm going to get huge. I am my body, and how that looks is everything. I have to be perfect. I have to be in control. I'll never be happy unless I'm thinner." Then ask of each thought you've written down, "Is it true?"

Notice in these examples how a negative meaning is given to the simple fact that you weigh a certain number of pounds. Many of these statements are stories about what gaining weight will mean to the *you* that you imagine yourself to be. These stories are false because they're predicated on concepts such as *good, bad, ugly, fat, horrible,* and *perfect* and assume to know something that isn't true or can't be known.

What needs to be exposed in any exploration of your thoughts is not only a thought's falseness, but also its hidden emotional content and the ego's agenda. "I'm getting fat" is loaded emotionally without appearing to be. If a friend said, "You're getting fat," that would be considered judgmental, offensive, hurtful, and unacceptable from a friend. So why would you accept this from your own mind? You would, only if you believed that judgment had some value, if you believed you needed it to be a better person.

Do such thoughts make you a better person? Thoughts like that make you feel bad and small, and when people feel that way, they don't become better people. Unhappy people who don't feel good about themselves tend to become even more lost in their thought-stream and closed down to life. When you don't love yourself, you don't feel much love for others or for life. Your love and creative juices don't flow. You remain stuck in the ego, which is exactly what the ego wants. That is the ego's underlying agenda.

"I'm getting fat" is a good example of a thought that accomplishes what the ego usually sets out to do. The ego's agenda is to create a sense of having a problem, of something lacking, or of not being good enough. This results in desires and feelings that, then, drive actions. If you believe such thoughts, the ego's got you, and your life is in its hands. That is its agenda. The more attention you give such thoughts, the more frequently they arise, and the more believable they seem.

As you examine the thoughts in your thought-stream, be sure to also notice this agenda. Thoughts are not what they appear to be. Most exist for the purpose of maintaining the ego. They come from the ego and serve the ego. The ones that don't are few and far between, easy to dismiss, and don't create negative feelings.

This is just one example of how a judgmental thought can affect you adversely, but most other thoughts are no different. When you look closely at your thoughts, you discover that most of them make you feel bad. If a thought does that, the ego is behind it, and you don't need that thought.

The thoughts that arise most frequently are the ones you believe most strongly. Those are the ones that will need the most investigation. The most frequent thoughts are also likely to have an emotional component, giving them power over how you think about yourself and how you behave. These are the types of thoughts that shape and control people's lives. Without serious investigation, they are unlikely to diminish significantly.

These are also the thoughts that define the false self and limit you. Without them, you would still be the character you're meant to be, with the personality, drives, quirks, preferences, and talents of that character; but you'd be a happy character, not a miserable one. And you'd be a kind character, not an unkind one. The qualities of your divine self would shine through this character instead of being blocked by the clouds of the false self. In other words, you'd be your best self. By not identifying with the thought-stream, all you lose are images and ideas of a false self, not anything you ever needed to play the role you're meant to play in this life.

Once you've seen the uselessness and destructiveness of most of your thoughts, you can get beyond resisting them or being irritated by them by realizing one important thing: Your thoughts aren't personal. They don't mean anything about you—the real you, that is. All of humanity has the same thoughts, and they're responsible for all the suffering in the world. Once you realize this, the only sensible response to egoic thoughts is accepting that they are part of life and having compassion for this very human challenge.

If only this realization could be had simply by reading this! Unfortunately, this realization usually takes time to sink in deeply. As your thoughts weaken and the ability to witness them develops, your thoughts *become* more impersonal. Once that happens, the impersonal nature of thought is much easier to see. Before then, you can remind yourself that your thoughts are not yours, and that will lay the groundwork for a deeper realization.

The Impersonal Nature of Thoughts

Thoughts are not personal means they are impersonal, universal. The thought-stream is similar from one person to another, with only minor variations. Just as some people have blue eyes instead of brown, some have more of certain kinds of thoughts than others. But thoughts, regardless of what they are, serve the same two purposes. First, they define you: They tell you who you are, how you look, how you feel, how you compare to others, and how you're seen by others. Second, they tell you what to do and how to behave: what you can and cannot do, what you should and should not do, and how to behave. The specific definitions and instructions vary, but everyone is given basic definitions and instructions. This is your programming, your software.

This programming comes partly from genetics and partly from conditioning, or programming acquired from the environment, particularly from those who raised you or with whom you grew up. And where did their definitions and instructions come from? The same place: from their genetics and their environment.

Given this, you can probably appreciate that your conditioning is not necessarily that useful or true now. If you look at the specific definitions and instructions about who you are and how you should behave, you can see they are arbitrary. They could apply to anyone, although the truth is, they apply to no one, really.

So much has happened within society in even just the last one hundred years, and yet similar conditioning continues to be passed down from one generation to the next. To say that some of it is outmoded would be an understatement. Because conditioning hasn't kept up with evolution, it's causing a lot of problems. People continue to believe things that aren't true, such as the superiority of certain races and religions, and they behave in ways that are dysfunctional, such as trying to solve problems through war and terrorism. Conditioning that may have been appropriate or useful for one era is now contributing to humanity's demise. This is no less true on a personal level. Much of your conditioning doesn't contribute to your well-being but does the opposite. Seeing this is important now.

The ego is an antiquated aspect of the human machinery. It developed to support survival when humanity lived in tribal groups and hunted and foraged for food. Then, danger lurked everywhere, and fear enabled humans to avoid being prey. The ego's motto was and still is "Kill or be killed." However, now, in most cases, fear has nothing to do with an actual threat but is caused by a thought. Fearful thoughts cause people to be stressed-out, make poor decisions, and do unspeakable things to each other. Fear that stems from believing mistaken thoughts is at the root of most bad and ill-advised behavior, and such fear comes from the primitive ego.

The voice in your head is not functional, even though it may have been and even though some remnant of ego is still needed to function and survive. This is an important distinction: You need an ego, but you don't need the voice in your head, which is the ego taking over the mind. Your evolution as a species depends on recognizing the destructiveness of this voice.

The thoughts in your thought-stream are not your friend. Seeing this can work against you, however, if it pits you against your thoughts. "What you resist persists," and so resistance is not a useful stance. Thoughts are not the enemy, although once you realize the truth about them, it's natural to feel that way. However, only the ego could see anything as an enemy.

An enemy is someone you fear, someone you believe has power over you. But thoughts are not to be feared, as they have no power over you if you don't believe them. Would you be afraid of a rope if you knew it was a rope and not a snake? The same is true of thoughts. They are what they are, an outmoded part of the human machinery. If you leave them alone, they'll go away. Leaving them alone is enough.

This is easy enough to do if you don't believe that your thoughts mean anything about you, if you know they aren't really yours. The only way they could bother you is if you believed in the *you* they describe. To the extent that you believe in this *you*, there will be a reaction to your thoughts—either buying in to them or being irritated that they still arise. So, what to do?

The answer is simple: Just notice. Notice the irritation, annoyance, or desire to be rid of thoughts. That isn't the real you that feels that way. The real you is loving this great adventure called life, including the challenge of having thoughts that are both entrancing and unwanted. What an interesting dilemma being human is! When you accept your thoughts and let them be, you drop into Presence, where seeing the truth about them is much easier.

You can see there is a Catch-22 here: You need some distance from thoughts before you can be objective enough to see the truth about them and detach from them completely. This distance develops over time, and there's only so much you can do to develop this. Daily meditation speeds this along like nothing else because it teaches you to notice thoughts. Meditation develops the Noticer because meditation brings you into Presence, which is what notices and experiences life.

The Practice of Noticing

Noticing is the powerful spiritual practice of letting everything be as it is, as Presence does. The practice of noticing is silent witnessing, devoid of any mental or emotional content, such as opinions, desires, judgments, comparisons, preferences, or other hooks that draw you into the ego's world. It is simple experiencing without taking a stand. Noticing is definitely not interesting to the ego!

To call noticing a practice makes it into something to do, when noticing is actually always going on, although often below one's awareness. To do this practice, all you really have to *do* is notice that noticing is already happening. Simply notice what is noticing. Noticing the Noticer lands you in Presence.

Even when you're lost in thought, at some point, you notice you are, and you return to noticing the room you're in, the sky, the bird's song, the car noise, or whatever might be going on in your environment. Then you slip back into the illusory world of thought again until you notice reality again. No matter how much time you've spent lost in thought, the Noticer has been there all along. That Noticer is what's been experiencing your life all along. It is who you really are.

Noticing is the alternative to being lost in thought. Once your capacity to be aware and to witness thoughts is sufficiently developed, you can choose to notice your thoughts instead of identify with them. You can notice a thought arising or catch yourself involved in thoughts. Then you can choose to be present by turning your attention to your body and senses, your breath, or your environment—to something in the here and now. Notice what else is here besides thoughts and the feelings those thoughts produce. Notice what are you seeing, hearing, sensing, or experiencing in some other way. What is this moment like without thought? That is the experience of Presence.

Noticing is Presence's experience of life, which is a much better experience than the one you have when you're identified with the thought-stream. All of the judgments, desires, fears, worries, opinions, and comparisons that are part of the story of *me and my life* are not that much fun. The ego enjoys them, but you really don't. Fortunately, once you realize there is an alternative, you can choose to give your attention to your sensory experience. If you stay in your body and senses long enough, you'll drop into Presence, which is having a wonderful time.

You are a mystery, aren't you? Sometimes you are Presence, sometimes you are what you imagine yourself to be, sometimes you are your ego, and sometimes you are what is choosing between these! You are actually all of these. There is really only one you, but it identifies with and alternates between these different aspects of being.

Noticing unravels everything that holds the ego's world together: judgments, comparisons, desires, beliefs, opinions, fantasies, worries, fears, and every other kind of feeling or thought. Noticing brings objectivity to these and a capacity to know the truth about them and, most importantly, choice. The ego's world cannot withstand this kind of scrutiny.

In spite of one's best intentions to not identify with thought, some thoughts will be so deeply believed that identification will happen automatically, and any feelings related to those thoughts may compound that identification. Objectivity and your ability to choose will be lost for a while. This is normal and not a problem. You wouldn't be human if you didn't have some thoughts that had this kind of power. Eventually you'll see through even those thoughts before they have a chance to catch you up. Until then, noticing will help dissolve these more compelling thoughts too. Whenever you do finally notice you're feeling bad, simply notice you are noticing this. Then Presence is back online and can be used to experience those feelings more fully and investigate the underlying thoughts.

Working with Feelings

Here is an excerpt from *From Stress to Stillness: Tools for Inner Peace* by this author about what to do when you are gripped by difficult feelings:

> "Many of our feelings come from the hurt child that lives within us in our unconscious, and they come up whenever something triggers that emotional complex in the unconscious. Such feelings are healed by being with them with acceptance and curiosity, just as a good and loving parent might be with a hurt child. Without such a relationship to these feelings, they'll continue to be triggered and are likely to be reinforced and even strengthened rather than healed, as we act them out in the usual dysfunctional ways.
>
> Just as children need a patient, attentive, loving, and compassionate parent to soothe them when they are hurting, our feelings need us to listen to them patiently, compassionately, and lovingly. To heal and evolve, our

feelings need us to just sit with them quietly, experience them, accept them, listen to them, and send love to them. This acceptance and receptivity towards feelings is often provided by a therapist or other healer or even a very good friend. But in many cases, we can provide this for ourselves.

In order to be with our feelings in a way that heals them, we first have to dis-identify with them. To dis-identify, we have to stop in the midst of feeling whatever we're feeling and notice that we're feeling something. Noticing that we're having a feeling and then making an intention to dis-identify with and heal it brings us into a new relationship with the feeling. We've taken a step back from the feeling, and now we're witnessing it. Now we have some choice about what to do next. We don't have to go back into identification and act out the feeling in the usual ways. We can relate to it from some distance.

It's important at this point that we relate to the feeling with compassion and not hostility or rejection. We bring compassion to the part of us that is experiencing this feeling, while staying in touch with the part that is able to witness the feeling and just be with it. Relating to the feeling from a place of a compassionate witness is what heals it. This compassionate witness is our true self, while the hurting self is the human self. We are compassionate towards our human self, while recognizing that it isn't who we really are.

As part of this process of dis-identification, it's helpful to keep stepping back into a broader awareness that includes not only the feeling but everything else that is present, because when we're identified with a feeling, that feeling looms large and blocks out the rest of reality. We can easily get sucked back into identification if we don't make a conscious effort at this point to move further into a more expanded awareness.

To help bring the rest of reality into focus and put the feeling in its proper perspective, we can ask ourselves: 'Is there space around the feeling? How big is that space? Can I make that space even bigger? What is that space like? Is peace there? Is love there? Is compassion there? Can I be that space? What's it like to observe the feeling from the perspective of space? As space, what can I discover about this feeling? Can I, as space, give love and compassion to the feeling?'

When we do this, we discover that there's plenty of room in this wide-open spacious awareness for everything and every emotion, no matter how big a feeling may be. When we're able to identify with the spaciousness instead of with the feeling, the feeling is seen in perspective and seen for what it is—a feeling that comes and goes. It's just the conditioning we were given. We see that that feeling doesn't harm or affect who we really are: the spacious awareness in which the feeling is showing up. Because we see that having this feeling doesn't mean that there's something wrong with us, we can just let it be there, witness it, and get curious about it.

From that spaciousness, we can allow ourselves to fully have the experience of that emotion in our body without any story about it. We can let the feeling be as big as it is and as it needs to be. We can experience how it feels in the body, where it's felt in the body, what it has to say, and what it wants and needs. We can find out all about it. We don't need to change or fix the feeling in any way. We only need to be with it compassionately and let it be as it is.

When we simply sit with a feeling this way, any insight we need about the feeling will naturally arise, particularly insight into the beliefs that are behind the feeling. Sitting with a feeling this way is like listening to it. Our acceptance and receptivity open up the feeling, which relaxes, opens, and expresses itself, as it finally has our loving attention.

As the belief or beliefs behind a feeling are revealed, we accept these beliefs and have compassion for our humanness and the natural tendency to form mistaken beliefs. And we forgive ourselves for hurting ourselves by holding such beliefs. We may also need to forgive others, such as our parents, who taught us these mistaken beliefs. These individuals unconsciously and, therefore, innocently passed on their own misunderstandings and wounds. Forgiving ourselves and others helps us put these mistaken beliefs behind us.

When a belief behind a feeling is clearly seen, what often follows is a flood of tears. This release of feelings feels good, like a cleansing, and is often fairly short-lived. There is a cleanness about these tears, with no feeding them on the part of the mind. They suddenly come and just as suddenly end. Such tears are part of the healing and a sign that we have gotten to a core truth behind the feeling. Afterwards, as with a storm that has ended, the sun peeks through the clouds and we feel at peace. All is right with the world once again." (*From Stress to Stillness,* pp. 163-166)

From Stress to Stillness also has some very helpful information about meditation and other spiritual practices, not mentioned here, which will help you be in Presence.

The Practice of Silence

Another very valuable spiritual practice is keeping silent. Being silent for seconds, minutes, hours, days, or weeks is a time-honored practice for breaking identification with one's thoughts. This is because one of the biggest reinforcers of the thought-stream is speech. Giving voice to thoughts fortifies them like nothing else. Whenever you stop yourself from saying something you would ordinarily say, you're making a conscious choice to extinguish that thought. Over time, making that choice will weaken the potency of the entire thought-stream.

Even keeping silent for just a few seconds before speaking will make your interactions with others deeper and more meaningful, as the thought-stream is less likely to be mindlessly indulged in. Not filling the space with idle chatter leaves space for Presence to enter and either speak through you, through the other person, or just be there.

Keeping silent for longer periods, for days or weeks, is an even more powerful practice. That's when you can really begin to conquer the habit of speaking whatever is on your mind. After keeping silent for a week or more, often in spiritual retreats, many have their first experience of Presence and a quiet mind.

By not giving voice to your thoughts and by taking a break from other people's thoughts, such as those on TV, thoughts lose some of their power over you. They can be seen more clearly and objectively, as just thoughts. It becomes clear that most of the thoughts you've given voice to have never been your true voice or even your character's true voice, but the thought-stream's, the ego's.

The objectivity gained from practicing silence means more choice around your thoughts, more space. More space around your thoughts means more Presence and more ability to see the truth about them. This is how silence unravels the ego's world. One by one, thoughts drop away, out of the thought-stream, until there is more and more space in between thoughts.

At a certain point, Presence overwhelms the power of the thought-stream, and you realize the truth: You *are* Presence. When you know yourself as the Presence within which the false self, its thoughts and feelings, and everything else arise instead of the *you* who occasionally experiences Presence, that's called self-realization, or awakening.

An important aspect of the practice of silence is taking a break from conversations, TV, the news, movies, the internet, and other forms of mental entertainment and stimulation. Listening to other people's egoic minds in the media or elsewhere can draw you into the ego's world and reinforce the false self as much as listening to your own mind can.

Once you're more stabilized in Presence, movies, the news, TV, and the like can be appreciated from Presence. You might enjoy observing human nature and feel the same enjoyment of life while watching a movie that Presence feels in living your life. On the other hand, you might find yourself much less interested in these things. Once you know yourself as Presence, certain entertainments lose their allure.

To flourish, one's spiritual life requires alone time, space, and quiet, including a break from stimulating the mind. To touch into and cultivate the Silence within, silence is necessary. What you do in this silence is simply notice whatever is showing up in the Silence. You make space and then see what arises in that space, which is the space from which all life springs.

Making room for Silence might mean sitting and simply noticing your thoughts without engaging in them, which is a type of meditation. Or you might sit outside and gaze at the trees or sky. Or you might take a walk in nature, listen to music, or simply lie on the sofa or in bed. The important thing is that these activities take you into Presence and not further into your thoughts about yourself. Thinking about oneself often passes as self-exploration, self-analysis, or self-examination, but notice the common word in all of these: self.

Making a conscious choice to make room for Silence in your life and to stop speaking, even briefly, sends a message to your unconscious that you're in charge, not it. Doing this also sends a message to the nonphysical beings guiding you. The message is that you are ready to move beyond ego identification. Once you give evidence of this and of your openness to their help, help is given.

Nonphysical beings can help in a number of ways. They can clear some of the emotional content of your thoughts, lessening their impact. They can also remove and keep away negative nonphysical influences, entities and thought-forms, which hold negative thoughts and addictions in place. Most importantly, within the space of Presence opened up by practicing silence, you'll be able to receive intuitive messages from these helpers more easily.

You are always watched over and assisted by these beings in whatever you choose to do. If you choose to be involved in your thoughts, that is respected, and the beings guiding you allow you to have that experience. When you choose something else, they help you have that experience. They are forever by your side, helping you navigate and learn from whatever experience you've chosen.

Choosing to wake up from the madness of the mind is a momentous shift in a human life. In such transitions, people often make other changes as well: in relationships, career, and how they spend their time. New energy, both physical and spiritual, comes in, which opens up new possibilities. What happens next with such spiritual openings is anyone's guess, and those assisting you on etheric levels adjust accordingly. Heaven rejoices when people begin to wake up. Embodying the divine self is the culmination of your earthly lifetimes, so celebration is in order.

Exercising your power to choose silence or any other activity that promotes Presence is a real turning point on the path to spiritual liberation. This marks an acceleration in your spiritual growth, which will reverberate in your life in countless ways. Things will change, many of them unexpected. Anything truly begins to be possible. More conscious choosing of Presence lays the groundwork for Grace to be more active in your life. The more sincere you are, the more Grace is bestowed.

Overcoming Roadblocks to Silence

When you begin a practice of silence, whether that's being more silent in your everyday life or taking a day or more to be silent, the mind will try to undermine your efforts with certain thoughts: "It's too hard." "It isn't necessary." "It won't matter." "This is silly." "You're being impolite." "You're being unsociable." "People won't like you." "People will think you're strange." Just notice such thoughts and remind yourself that every effort to be silent or to speak only when necessary *does* matter and benefits everyone. Whatever is good for your spiritual well-being must also be good for everyone else in the Whole.

The mind doesn't want you to disengage from it or other mentally stimulating activities or to be silent with others. Just notice all the ways the mind tries to involve you in thinking, speaking, and activities that stir up your emotions, such as news, blogs, TV, twitter, magazines at the grocery counter, radio talk shows, gossip, and other vehicles of melodrama. Notice how attracted the mind is to opinions, judgments, gossip, how people look, who's up and who's down, stories, and drama.

One of the mind's favorite ways to engage you is by bringing up emotionally charged memories: losses and tragic events (even ones you've only heard about or seen on TV), upsetting things people said or did, or times when you were struggling or sick. Or the mind might bring up fears about the future: What if you lose your job? What if your spouse dies? What if something happens to your child? What if you get cancer? Thoughts such as these are the "big guns" the mind hauls out to get you involved with it. Just notice this, laugh, and return to Presence. In that noticing lies freedom.

The mind might also try to scare you into believing you'll lose or upset relatives and friends if you are more silent and present when you're with them. Or if that doesn't work, it might attempt to make you feel proud or superior for being silent and imply that those who are more ego-bound than you are "unevolved" or "don't get it." The mind is very tricky, and you'll have to keep noticing the ways it tries to keep you involved with it.

It is true that being more silent and making more room for Presence in your life in other ways will most likely change how you are in relationships and how you want to spend your time. You may lose interest in social gatherings and idle chitchat, and your friends might feel hurt by your lack of engagement.

However, the changes you're going through aren't personal. They're the expression of an evolutionary movement within you and ultimately within everyone, and they can't be helped. Things change, and you have to accept this, and so do others.

You can't let feelings of guilt keep you tied to outworn relationships. Guilt is one of the ways the ego keeps people in old patterns: by keeping them in relationships that pull them into those patterns. Becoming more present is bound to result in making more conscious choices about your relationships and how you spend your time. If you don't make such choices, you risk returning to a more ego-bound state.

Making changes in your relationships can be very challenging. How do you move away from people and activities you were once involved with? There's no formula for how to do this. In some cases, you just say, "No thank you" to invitations and give a polite excuse. There's no need to hurt feelings or set yourself against others. Explanations are best worded with "I" instead of "you": "I'm feeling like being alone these days." "I need to take care of some things at home." "I'm not that interested in that." Statements with "you" in them should be avoided: "You're stuck in your ego." "You aren't supportive." "You aren't growing." "You don't understand." "You aren't open enough."

The important thing is to be true to your own Heart, to what you feel moved to do or not do, and to what brings you joy. Let joy be your guide in all things. If you feel a surge of joy arise in your Heart at the prospect of doing something or being with someone, then follow that joy. If not, where might joy lie? What do you really want? One of the greatest benefits of practicing silence is that it is in Silence that answers to these important questions arise, although not in words. It turns out, the mind never did have those answers.

CHAPTER 5

The Purified Human Being

What Remains in the Mind

When the clouds of egoic negativity have been cleared because you're identifying with your thought-stream so little, you feel like you do when the sky is brilliant blue: buoyant, carefree, fresh, alive, and embracing of life. The result of disengaging from the thought-stream is that you're a happy and genuinely nice human being, not because you want people to like you or you want something else from them, but because the love you feel naturally expresses itself as kindness and attentiveness to others.

Even though there's little identification with your egoic mind, you still have a certain personality, a unique style, drives, and desires that support your character's life purpose. On the surface, you appear as unique as ever, although in your essence, you have never been unique. The same divine self is living through everyone and everything. Just as each finger is unique but not separate from the hand, each character is unique but not separate from the Whole. And as each of the fingers is moved by the same hand, every character is moved by the same force.

Once one's relationship with the egoic mind has been transformed by having seen through the mind, the result is a more purified human being, cleansed of much of the ego's useless negativity, lies, limiting stories, impulses, feelings, and tendencies. The character no longer automatically adopts the ego's point of view and now sees life through the divine self's eyes more consistently. Instead of judgment, lack, fear, and dissatisfaction, the character experiences clarity, joy, wonder, awe, gratitude, peace, and love. Who wouldn't be a better human being, given such a transformation of perception?

When the thought-stream is no longer believed, the ego-driven human being becomes a divinely-driven human being. The character has a new master. When this happens, what remains in the mind are:

1. **Residual egoic thoughts**, which are generally disregarded. There may always be some egoic thoughts in the thought-stream, but the ones that remain hold little sway and have little effect. They carry on in the background, like a poorly-tuned and uninteresting radio station. Giving that station attention tunes it in, while ignoring it tunes it out.

   No one is perfectly tuned out, however, as anyone can get caught in the ego again. The ego is a powerful force in human existence. Just when you think it's extinguished or rendered impotent, it can be reborn under a new identity. The "I" that used to be unworthy or unhappy can become "spiritual," "enlightened," "awake," or improved in some other way. But it is still the "I." It may be a new, better, and more subtle identity, but it's still an identity.

2. **Neutral thoughts, which are mostly commentary on the obvious.** When your mind is clear of the more noxious

egoic thoughts, you'll notice how much it comments on what's already happening and already known, as if it's telling you something you don't already know: "We're out of milk." "She didn't see me." "The sky is really blue today." "I need to brush my teeth." "It's getting dark." "It's time to walk the dog." You didn't need to think those thoughts to know those things. But such thoughts are harmless, in that they don't stir up negative feelings. They're often the kinds of things people share to be sociable or communicate information.

3. **Positive thoughts that express the love, gratitude, and happiness that flow through you from the divine self:** "What a beautiful day it is!" "I'm so happy to discover this." "It's the perfect dress!" "I love how you said that." "That was the best lasagna ever." "I can't thank you enough." "I love this!"

   Although it's natural to want to express the joy and love that the divine self feels, even such positive expressions can be used by the ego to feel special, the implication being: "Aren't I wonderful for being so loving! Aren't I amazing for creating such a great life!" If you feel yourself spin out into a high, that's probably the ego, as the hallmark of the divine self is equanimity. Its happiness is more subtle and doesn't need to be declared to others.

4. **Humorous thoughts.** An emptier mind allows you to take life, including the ego, more lightly and enjoy it. You might find yourself making funny observations about life and about the ego. When people say, "People are funny," they're pointing to this kind of good-spirited humor.

5. **Thoughts you're consciously choosing to think because it serves some purpose.** Rather than the egoic mind using you, you're using the mind as the mind is meant to be used, as a tool for intelligent thinking. The rational mind is an immense gift and a great pleasure to exercise, and you're meant to use it and enjoy it. You might use it to explore a feeling, examine whether something is true, study something, explore a creative idea or possibility, consider how you might do something, wonder why something is the way it is, or find a solution to some practical problem.

The difference between these practical or exploratory types of thoughts and ego-driven thought is that thinking them serves a purpose, and they're absent of "I" and an egoic agenda. You can feel the difference between practical or exploratory thoughts and ones that belong to the voice in your head. If for any reason, thinking makes you feel bad, you can be sure the ego is behind those thoughts and has hijacked the rational thinking process.

In everyone's mind, egoic thoughts are mixed in with more rational, neutral, and positive ones. As a result, being involved in any kind of intellectual or rational mental activity can be a slippery slope, landing you unexpectedly and unconsciously in ego-based thought. The line can easily become blurred between the rational and irrational, as the mind goes from objective thinker into a whiny complainer, judge, or blamer. For instance, something as ordinary as buying an airline ticket can turn into a rant against the airlines and an experience of "poor me, nothing ever goes well." The ego can use any kind of mental activity to draw you into its world of dissatisfaction.

Intellectual and more rational types of individuals are at somewhat of an advantage in keeping the ego at bay since their minds are already so full of intellectual thoughts, leaving less room for the ego's voice. Rational types also see more clearly than most that this voice is illogical and emotionally inflammatory and, so, are not tricked so easily by it. However, the drawback is that more intellectual and rational types may have difficulty moving out of their mind and into their body and senses. So although these individuals may not be overtaken by the egoic mind as easily as some, they might not be very present or give credence to the more subtle realm of the divine self or trust it. As a result, experiencing Presence and its guidance can be more challenging for them.

Rational types often equate the more subtle, intuitive realm, what some call transrational, with the ego's world of emotion and irrationality. This misunderstanding can keep them from being open to a richer way of experiencing life than through their intellect. Rational types often don't get beyond this misunderstanding without the "gift" of suffering or some other eye-opening event, such as a near-death experience or some other psychic or spiritual experience.

When the mind is being used intelligently and functionally, it is actually the divine self that is using it. The divine self has used your mind this way countless times throughout your life, since the divine self is what is living your life. The divine self steps aside at times and lets you follow the ego's desires and ideas if you choose. But when you aren't doing that, you're doing what the divine self is moving you to do. The divine self isn't separate from you or your life in any way. It is life itself living through you when you allow it to. When you're aligned with the divine self in this way, you are following your Heart.

Following Your Heart

Everyone knows what follow your heart means. It's a common expression and an everyday experience. Many times a day, even in ego-driven lives, people follow their Heart. They can't help it because the Heart is very compelling. It moves you, pulls you, drives you, encourages you, and inspires you — wordlessly. For example, even the most self-absorbed person might suddenly, without thinking about it, stop in the midst of rushing somewhere to hand a few dollars to a homeless person.

The Heart I am referring to is the spiritual heart. It is not something off in some other dimension but right here and experienced by everyone. The spiritual heart has nothing to do with the difficult emotions of the human heart, which are the result of believing your thoughts. The emotions of the spiritual heart, if you could call them that, are love, joy, gratitude, and peace. These aren't emotions in the usual sense but qualities of the divine self and indicators of being aligned with it. Whenever the divine self is operating through you, you feel love, joy, gratitude, and peace, although often only very subtly.

When people experience their heart being open, this is the spiritual heart and the experience of Presence. As with "follow your heart," people generally know what an open heart is. It is the experience of feeling loving, accepting, compassionate, and open to life and others. A profound experience of an open heart is sometimes accompanied by tears that feel good and cleansing.

Although the Heart is often overridden by the egoic mind, when the Heart is followed, the reward is good feelings and positive results. It is the Heart that draws people out of the egoic trance, since the Heart is the alternative to listening to the voice in your head and a much more rewarding choice.

Eventually people realize that the Heart is the true and reliable master.

Following the Heart can be challenging because the Heart doesn't communicate in words, but through the body. It does this through:

❖ Urges to act,

❖ A sense of "yes" or rightness about a particular direction,

❖ Motivation and enthusiasm for a particular direction,

❖ Inspired ideas, and

❖ Spontaneous actions that just happen without thought.

In these ways, the Heart shows you which way to go and which way not to go. The Heart also communicates through events and people showing up in your life that bring opportunities, jobs, information, gifts, money, relationships, creative ideas, help, encouragement, and other forms of support. The Heart may also communicate by taking something away: a job, a spouse, a capability, a house, or some other valued part of your life. Removing something from your life may be necessary to steer your life in a new direction.

If you examine the things you do during the day, you'll realize that many of your actions are inspired or spontaneous and that these actions are the most easeful, productive, and satisfying of your day. As your human self becomes more purified of ego, these types of actions fill more of your day.

Actions that follow from your mind may be productive, but they often don't feel easeful, enjoyable, or fulfilling. They also may not lead to anything but achieving certain egoic goals.

Actions that come from the divine self, on the other hand, support a greater plan, one that is deeply satisfying and rewarding when followed.

This plan is your life's purpose, and this purpose also serves the Whole in some, often mysterious, way. You know when you're aligned with your life's purpose by feelings of joy, peace, contentment, fulfillment, and satisfaction. You know when you're not, by depression or an overall dissatisfaction with your life. This is tricky, however, because the ego's nature is to be dissatisfied. So even if you are fulfilling your life's purpose, if you're listening to your egoic mind a lot, you're probably dissatisfied a lot. However, it's much more likely that if you're involved with the ego to that extent, you're also not aligned with your life's purpose.

If you are aligned, there will be a spring in your step, a sense of aliveness, an excitement about life, and a feeling of rightness about what you're doing, which will shore you up even if other things in your life are challenging. The beauty of being aligned with the divine self is that you enjoy what you're doing, you're fulfilled by it, and you have the courage to overcome any obstacles related or unrelated to it. And when you feel this good, you're not so likely to cave in to the egoic mind's negativity.

The opposite is also true, of course: When you aren't aligned with your life's purpose, you'll feel dissatisfied and possibly depressed. This makes you vulnerable to other negative thoughts and feelings and susceptible to addictive behaviors. This, in turn, makes you even more subject to negativity.

Often this negative cycle is broken as a result of some kind of crisis: losing your job, a spouse leaving, becoming ill, or losing money. Any of these might be a wake-up call from the divine self and an opportunity to rebuild your life anew. When the structures in your life crumble, that's the right experience. Things change because it's time for them to change. When such things happen, you have to be willing to see them as an opportunity for something new to be born and created by you.

When structures fall apart, it's important to ask, "What do I really want? What's really important to me? What excites and interests me? Where is my joy?" These kinds of questions point you to your Heart's desire.

Two things are going on in any moment: What your ego desires and what your Heart desires. They may or may not be the same thing. In times of crisis, your ego probably wants whatever was lost to not be lost or it wants that replaced. But wanting what life has taken away is a waste of energy. If things are changing, then that must be what the Heart wants.

So when structures fall apart, it's also time to ask, "What does life want?" and look to see where life might be pointing you to next. Given the changes, what is possible now that wasn't possible before? Where is the flow going? What is showing up in the flow? What events? What opportunities? What urges and inspiration? What information? What people? Those things are how the divine self points you to what comes next.

Moment by moment, the divine self reveals its plan. You may have to pay close attention to see that something new is unfolding, and it may take a while for the new path or a new life to be revealed. But by "following the breadcrumbs" moment by moment, the way is revealed and the new life that is trying to be born will become more evident.

Isn't this how life has always unfolded? You've never known where your life is going. You follow this thought, that urge, this opportunity, that feeling, this intuition, that inspiration, this information, that person. Then one day, you see why you did all those things. They were leading somewhere; you just didn't realize it at the time.

Thoughts may or may not be a problem in this process of discovery. Ideas about what you *should* do can sidetrack or slow down the process, but life has a way of bringing you back on track even if your mind is trying to take you somewhere else. Most people have enough contact with their divine self that they are living out some version of their life's purpose. This purpose might have been compromised somewhat by the egoic mind, but most people are able to fulfill their life's purpose to some extent within the structures co-created by their egoic mind and divine self.

Most people's lives are a co-creation between the ego and the divine self. To the extent that one's life reflects the divine self more than the ego, it will be happier, easier, and more fulfilling. Those who are choosing against the divine flow, however, will find themselves running into more than their share of difficulties, frustrations, and blocks. The divine self has ways of bringing about its plan in spite of the ego, and it will use crises, blocks, and other difficulties to do so.

To a more rational mind, the idea that a greater intelligence is behind life and shaping it may seem extremely irrational and even silly. People don't always get what they deserve, and just as often, things fall in people's laps for no reason. To the mind, life seems irrational, random, and out of control. But the mind isn't privy to the bigger picture. If it were, it would see magnificent intelligence.

You are definitely not in control of the outcomes in your life and neither is anyone else, but not because life is random or meaningless. Something else other than your will is pulling the strings, and fortunately, it is very wise and knows exactly what everyone needs to fulfill his or her part in the Whole. Sometimes life delivers boons and sometimes challenges, but everything that happens is designed for the greater good of the Whole and to help you fulfill your life's purpose and learn whatever you need to for your evolution. There is intelligence behind the seeming inequities and randomness of life and a reason things happens as they do.

Trusting this will help you navigate the more difficult times, as you'll be able to see good even in adversity. Even if life were not this way, believing this, would be helpful. A positive attitude is very important in life. No matter what life delivers, if you focus on what you have rather than on what you've lost, you'll fare much better. The truth is, you always have a lot. Furthermore, life abhors a vacuum and will surely bring something new to fill any loss. However, you have to be willing to see the Grace in every event, or you might not notice it. Life has a plan for everyone. If you believe that and look for what that might be, you have a much better chance of aligning with it and being happy.

Here are some things to understand about the life purpose:

❖ You will discover your life's purpose and fulfill it by doing what you love and what you have a natural talent and personality makeup for.

❖ The character you are playing was designed for this purpose and given all the necessary programming.

❖ Your life's purpose is not necessarily what you do for work or as a career. It might relate to a talent or hobby, advancing or sharing knowledge, speaking out about or solving a problem for society, growing emotionally, healing a psychological issue or wound, being a healer, advancing spiritually, making a practical contribution to society, raising children, learning to love, inventing or creating something, serving others, bringing new ideas to society or to a field of endeavor, or balancing a karmic debt. This list is by no means exhaustive, as the life purpose may also relate to learning any number of lessons and developing certain traits and capabilities that are part of your evolution as a human being.

❖ You may fulfill your life's purpose without ever realizing what it is.

❖ If you are not fulfilling your life's purpose, you'll feel unhappy, unfulfilled, or depressed, unless it's something that isn't meant to be fulfilled until later.

❖ If your life's purpose is not fulfilled until later in life, then what you do earlier in your life will surely lead up to it, and that will be fulfilling in its own way.

❖ You made pre-life agreements with certain souls to help you with your life's purpose, and you agreed to help certain others with theirs. When the time is right, you'll meet those individuals, and that will feel very special.

❖ Your life's purpose will unfold in its own time. There is a plan, and it is in God's hands. Timing is everything. Patience and trust are often called for.

The Purified Personality

In speaking about purifying the human self of the ego, unfortunately the words pure and impure imply good and bad, and perfection and imperfection, which is not my intention. As I've said before, the human self will never be perfect, and there is nothing wrong with the ego. It is God-created to serve a purpose, and it does this very well.

To say that humanity needs to transcend the ego now is not to say that the ego is bad or evil. The ego is what it is and as it is meant to be. But for humanity to evolve more quickly, which is necessary now, the ego needs to take a backseat. The purpose of this teaching is to support that evolution, not for you to judge yourself or others for the ego that you and others can't help but have to the extent that you do.

What would your personality be like if it were more purified of ego? Another way of asking this is: What would your best human self be like? The question is not what would the perfect human be like, but *your* best self, given your personality. There is no one ideal human being. The best you can do is to be the best possible self you were programmed to be.

To discover what your best human self might look like, take a moment to consider how you would describe yourself. Write those descriptors down on a piece of paper. For instance, you might describe yourself as fickle, imaginative, cautious, responsible, perfectionistic, sensitive, unassertive, shy, hardworking, and impatient.

In examining the words you came up with for yourself, how many are actually describing the egoic self and not your best human self? For instance, if your personality were more purified of ego, you might not describe yourself as shy, since that implies some anxiety or fear. Introverted or private might be better words. *Fickle, impatient, unassertive,* and *perfectionistic* are other examples of descriptions of your egoic self; while *responsible, hardworking, cautious, sensitive,* and *imaginative* are more descriptive of your best self.

The negative descriptors are areas of your personality where the ego is distorting a positive potential. Becoming clear about where the ego is hiding in your own personality can be very helpful. Shyness, for instance, isn't really a flaw; it's introversion with a degree of fear. Likewise, unassertiveness isn't really a flaw; it's assertiveness distorted and blocked by fear. Examining what that fear is all about can be literally enlightening, as dissolving that fear can make more room for divine light to infuse the personality, the character.

Not every negative descriptor needs to be examined this deeply to be released from the ego's distortion. Sometimes becoming aware of the ego's presence is all it takes. For instance, once you're aware that arrogance is distorted confidence, you can watch for any arrogance whenever you notice yourself feeling or expressing something that resembles confidence. You can ask yourself where on that spectrum of confidence versus arrogance does what you are feeling or expressing lie.

Watch how the ego might take a feeling of confidence and turn it into boasting, or how it might turn love into smothering, caution into fear, compassion into sorrow, or enthusiasm into grandiosity. Once you are tuned in to the possibility of ego distortion, you can get good at catching the ego in action, and then make another choice.

A number of personality traits are listed below. You can add some of your own as you come up with them. In a given moment, you can ask yourself where you are on a particular spectrum. Language makes it seem like you are, for instance, either confident or not, or arrogant or not. But the truth is, there are many shades of gray not represented by a word and its opposite. The two words merely mark the ends of a spectrum.

Here is a list of the purified and unpurified versions of a number of personality traits, in other words, some personality trait spectrums:

persevering . . . . . stubborn

communicative . . . . . verbose or gossipy

outgoing . . . . . narcissistic

expressive . . . . . bombastic

enthusiastic . . . . . grandiose

vivacious . . . . . obnoxious or loud

fun-loving . . . . . indulgent

private . . . . . withdrawn or secretive

easygoing . . . . . easily led or passive

empathetic . . . . . hypersensitive

giving and generous . . . . . a victim or martyr

nurturing . . . . . smothering

nice . . . . . needy or disingenuous

caring . . . . . merged with others

compassionate . . . . . sorrowful

assertive . . . . . aggressive

commanding . . . . . tyrannical or bossy

courageous . . . . . foolhardy

confident . . . . . boastful or unrealistic

strong . . . . . bullying

thorough . . . . . compulsive

responsible . . . . . workaholic

discriminating . . . . . judgmental

careful and cautious . . . . . fearful

flexible . . . . . fickle

The human self when purified of ego is pretty wonderful! Everyone is essentially divine, and when the ego is stripped away, nothing is left but the divine shining through the character. The negative side of humanity is simply a distortion or impurity caused by the ego.

Every negative trait stems from a positive impulse. The workaholic, the smothering mom, the victim, the bully, the judge, the tyrant, the gossip, and the addict are all doing their best to do the right thing. They're doing their best to try to be happy. Even killing or harming others could be understood to be deeply distorted love, albeit love for oneself — an attempt at self-preservation.

Much of self-help literature is geared to purifying the personality and enhancing one's life, and that's a boon to everyone: Divine light can enter a positive mind more easily than a negative one, and a better *me* makes for a better citizen, friend, lover, and parent. To the extent that self-help makes it possible to accept yourself and eventually discover that you are the divine self, self-help is helpful. To the extent that self-help supports the ego by fostering rejection of one's human imperfections and over concern with perfecting the false self, it can interfere with contacting your true perfection: the divine self.

Self-help often doesn't go far enough. The real reason for purifying the personality of ego—for being your best self—is not to gain comfort, success, or even happiness for yourself, although you may well do that, but to make this a better world. For a deeper transformation to take place within you and in the world, the self-centeredness promoted by self-help has to be transcended. A deeper transformation can occur once you see that who you are is not the character that is and always will be imperfect, but actually the divine self dressed up as that. Once that is realized, the divine self can incarnate more fully. Then you naturally become the wonderful human being you were trying so hard to be.

There is a time for everything, and there is a time for improving the human self. The point is that once the divine incarnates more fully, the effort to become a better human being is not required to the extent it was because you just *are* a better human being, at least most of the time.

Pitfalls on the Spiritual Path

In service to understanding this great mystery of divine incarnation, or embodiment, it may be helpful to be aware of some of the pitfalls on the spiritual path. To begin with, although effort and vigilance regarding the ego are required to awaken from the ego, too much pushing and striving to be free of the ego can be a pitfall. Pushing and striving in regard to spiritual attainment, as with anything else, is a sign of the ego. The ego pushes to achieve some perfected state it imagines exists, and in this way, continues to cause suffering.

You will never be perfectly free of the ego. In any moment, a remnant of ego can always be found, if only in seed potential. If you go looking for the ego in your speech and behavior, you'll be able to find it a little, if not a lot. Finding it in others is especially easy! Do be on the lookout for the ego, but please be careful not to turn this teaching into a reason to be judgmental of yourself or others or self-righteous. That would surely mean your ego was back in charge.

The ego is programming, some of which you need. As long as you are in human form, the faults entailed in this programming have to be accepted and put up with. Even when much of your ego is gone, you will not always be patient, you will not always be kind, you will not always be sensitive, you will not always be courageous, and you will not always speak the highest truth. Do your best to be your divine self in the world, and love yourself even when you fail. And love others even when they fail. Sometimes the best and only thing you can do is forgive your imperfections and those of others and keep trying to do your best.

Another pitfall is going too far in the opposite direction: You might indulge your bad habits, addictions, and imperfections because you realize they have nothing to do with who you really are. Some who have some spiritual understanding or who've had some realization of the truth lose interest in refining their personality or don't care how they behave or what impact they might be having on others. They've seen the truth about the nature of reality, and to them, it can seem like what they do and how they behave doesn't matter. But it does!

If you are being dismissive, detached, or insensitive to others in your everyday life, you need to look at that and not just brush it off as "That's just my personality" or "That's their problem" or "It's all an illusion." Any indifference about how you behave or unkindness towards others is a sign the ego is back in charge. Such indifference is not nonattachment or spiritual freedom, but the ego corrupting one's spiritual understanding or co-opting one's spiritual attainment.

Some who've had a very deep realization of the truth feel they've transcended the human experience altogether. They may stop referring to themselves in the first person, as if their body-mind has nothing to do with them. For example, they might say, "This body is thirsty" or "From here the experience is...." Although this language may represent their experience more accurately than the usual language, not participating in common language is a subtle way the ego expresses a sense of superiority and creates separation from others and from life. Some people never get beyond this stage because they believe they've achieved the ultimate enlightened state, since extreme detachment from the world can feel that way to those experiencing this.

Although such detachment is a big relief from human suffering, any lack of interest in the world and lack of concern for others reflects a lack of spiritual integration. The integrated state is one of compassion and deep love for life in all its manifestations. Until the divine is embodied as fully as possible and life is fully embraced, the human experience is not complete. You have taken on a birth to be both human and divine.

Another pitfall is spiritual pretense, or pretending you are accepting, loving, and at peace when you're not. Many have some familiarity with Presence and have had glimpses of the deeper reality as a result of meditation or spiritual experiences. When that's lost or obscured by the ego, they may try to give the impression, either through their actions or their speech, that they're still in touch with Presence.

Some might feel the need to fake this because of some confusion around the difference between these temporary experiences and self-realization. Although experiences of Presence and spiritual experiences often have a profound impact on one's life, possibly even changing the course of one's life, they are temporary and do not result in a permanent shift to Presence as one's essential identity, as self-realization does. What these experiences do is give people a glimpse of Presence and the deeper reality, inspire people to pursue spiritual life, and pave the way for a more permanent realization.

Self-realization, or awakening, is a permanent shift in identity to that of the divine self. With self-realization, you no longer believe yourself to be the false self but are seated firmly in the divine self. Self-realization is realizing your essential identity as Presence and knowing this unshakably, beyond a doubt. It is not an intellectual realization, which is a common misunderstanding.

Self-realization cannot be achieved by the mind through any kind of examination or understanding. It cannot be achieved by you at all. *You* don't realize anything. The realization is that the *you* that you thought you were never did exist in the first place. Although spiritual practices prepare the ground for self-realization, it is Grace that delivers it when the time is right. Once you've had such a realization, it doesn't leave you.

Just to be clear, self-realization, or awakening, is only the beginning of what I am calling the *process* of enlightenment, which brings increasingly more divine light into the body. Of course, divine light filters into the human self before self-realization as well, but this process accelerates significantly after self-realization.

The process of enlightenment parallels the process of detachment from one's thought-stream and the emptying out of thoughts from the thought-stream. This emptying out makes room for the divine self to express itself through the human. The process of enlightenment is the process of divine incarnation, or embodiment of the divine self. Enlightenment, itself, as I'm defining it, is the completion of that process. Unfortunately, these terms aren't used consistently by spiritual seekers or even by many spiritual teachers. So confusion abounds.

Another difference between a spiritual experience and self-realization is that you generally wouldn't be able to function in the state you are in during a spiritual experience if that state were to continue. After self-realization, however, the state you remain in—Presence—is very ordinary and very functional. Spiritual seekers often mistakenly believe that self-realization or enlightenment is like a nonstop spiritual experience, when it is actually a very ordinary state. It is your natural state, not an altered state of consciousness.

Just as those who've had some experience of Presence might imitate being in Presence when they're not, spiritual seekers who've not had any such experience might try imitating those who have. Many have studied the teachings thoroughly enough and sat with enough teachers to know how someone who is awake or self-realized talks and behaves, and they may try to act accordingly.

Many of the practices given by spiritual teachers, such as the practices of gratitude and loving kindness, are actually descriptions of what someone who is self-realized naturally does. However, performing these practices is not the same thing as pretending to feel a certain way. These spiritual practices act as bridges, which take one into an authentic experience of gratitude and love.

The problem with pretending to feel grateful, loving, compassionate, accepting, or peaceful when you aren't is that this is not being authentic. When you're trying to act a certain way, you are not being present. Rather, you are trying to conform to an idea in your mind of how you think you should be. Only the ego would do that, most likely to try to gain approval or respect. If you were actually present instead of trying to match an image in your mind, gratitude, love, acceptance, compassion, and peace would be there genuinely. Although acting lovingly is certainly preferable to acting unlovingly, how much better it is if you can be that way authentically.

Being authentic, or being honest with yourself about what is arising in you in the moment, whether that be anger, grief, fear, or conceit, and being willing to look at that, is the way to achieving the more purified personality that one might be trying to fake. Being honest with yourself *and bringing awareness to that* will shed light on any blind spots where the ego might be hiding. As a shadow is dispersed in the light, so is the ego dissolved in the light of awareness. If you are being inauthentic, however, you are denying any ego that is there and hiding it from others. The trouble with this is that an unacknowledged ego cannot be dissolved.

Being authentic doesn't mean acting out your ego when ego is there. That is just indulgence. Being authentic means being willing to admit to and take a look at any ego that might be lurking in you. Presence is this willingness to look. This looking reveals what you might not want to see about yourself and frees you from it. If you aren't willing to be honest with yourself and look — and to be humbled by what you find — your spiritual unfoldment won't progress as quickly as it might.

The process of bringing more divine light into the body is one of continual humbling. Humility is a byproduct of the spiritual path and why humility is cultivated in the various spiritual traditions. What is humbled is, of course, the ego. This humbling, little by little, lowers the ego down from its perch. Although this hurts when it happens, the hurt doesn't last for long, as the rewards become obvious. That perch never did feel that good, and not having to maintain one's superiority is a great relief. Thus the ego is chipped away, one pretense or lie at a time.

The divine self is fine with the imperfections and messiness of being a human being. It loves the human experience. This is a grand drama, a grand duality: human and divine, learning to co-exist in one form, operating amongst other imperfect, evolving human beings. What a wonderful challenge the divine self has given itself to test its metal!

The divine self is never harmed by mistakes or even by the most unspeakable acts. Life is like a play that way: The characters love each other, hate each other, and sometimes even kill each other. And at the end of the play, they take off their costumes and go out for a drink! In the end, a good time was had by all.

This may sound insensitive to those who suffer so greatly in this grand drama, but please remember that you are not only the actors in the drama, but also the scriptwriter. It is your play. You are doing it all. No one is doing anything to you. You are the divine scriptwriter and the human actor.

The difference between a play and life is that, over the course of hundreds of lifetimes, the Divine succeeds in infusing its magnificence into each human character it plays. So unlike the actors in a play, who keep repeating the same drama, you evolve and become glorious by the end of all of your lifetimes. You become Christ-like, a master, free of the "villain" ego, which caused all the pain and suffering. In the end, the divine self shines. Life has a happy ending in store for everyone.

Overcoming Habits and Addictions

You might be surprised to learn that bad habits and addictions don't necessarily have to be overcome to awaken or become enlightened. They relate to one's conditioning and may not interfere with spiritual progress if they aren't too serious. Obviously, if an addiction controls your life and interferes with your ability to function, it will block self-realization and enlightenment.

However, as Chogyam Trungpa demonstrated, even alcoholism can, at least after some degree of realization, coexist with enlightenment. Although, how much more effective he might have been and how much more he might have contributed to the world had he not been alcoholic, no one will ever know. Certainly nicotine and food addictions do not prevent people from achieving enlightenment. In any event, bad habits and addictions are likely to diminish or drop away on their own the more Presence becomes a living reality.

Everyone knows what addiction is like. No one escapes the tendency for the body to become addicted to food and other substances. Food addiction is actually built into the human animal as a survival mechanism. People naturally seek and crave sweet and fatty foods, for instance, because they provide the calories needed for survival.

Drug addiction is built in as well. Drugs provide a certain relief and escape from human suffering, which human beings long for and sometimes need, as in the case of pain. Human beings are programmed to seek relief from pain and suffering, and nature has provided that relief in the form of foods and plant medicines.

If you are suffering from an addiction, it's not your fault. The body does get addicted, and the character you are playing may be addicted to some things, but *you* are never addicted. Even in the midst of the worst addiction, the divine self can shine through and be experienced. In many cases, that is the best hope for overcoming an addiction. Presence heals.

Serious addiction is a process of en-darkenment, as the mind and attention are taken over by the craving, and nothing else seems to matter. Any process of addiction starts with a level of darkness, of un-enlightenment, around some emotion or emotional experience that hasn't been sufficiently processed. An event that produces strong emotions makes people vulnerable to addiction. If those emotions aren't handled properly, which they often aren't because of a lack of skills for doing so, then addiction may develop as a means of coping with those repressed emotions, and emotions in general.

Not only is addiction not someone's fault, but repressed emotions are also not someone's fault. How could you be at fault for something you aren't conscious of? The nature of the unconscious is that you aren't conscious of it. How you coped with something is how your body coped with it. At the time, you didn't have enough awareness to cope with it any differently. Although it may be true that, had more awareness been available to you, healing might have happened and addiction might have been avoided, the truth is, it couldn't have been any other way than it was.

This is a roundabout way of suggesting you let go of any guilt around any addiction you might have. Guilt only keeps people tied to addiction. This statement might seem counterintuitive. Doesn't guilt keep people from doing the wrong thing? That's the party line, but guilt is actually one of the ego's fondest tools.

Guilt is how the ego keeps you in line, doing its bidding. If guilt served the divine self, that would be another thing, but guilt serves the ego. Sometimes the ego's values are similar to the divine self's, in which case the ego's guilt may appear to be a good thing. But often the ego's values are—well—the ego's and not the divine self's. They are based on lies, on ideas about how things *should* be.

How things should be is not how they actually are. That's why *should* is a lie. *Should* is a concept, a manufactured idea to keep people in line and following their conditioning. Some conditioning is useful and true, but much of it is not. Conditioning causes people to be inflexible and make choices that might not be best. While the Heart knows how to act in any moment, your conditioning does not, although it pretends to.

Guilt is the ego's friend because it keeps you feeling bad about yourself, and that keeps the false self in place. If there is anything the false self is, it's an unhappy self. Guilt is the way the ego makes you wrong and makes you feel unworthy of knowing yourself as the divine self. The ego does this because it doesn't want you to know your divine self.

Here's how the ego operates: It tells you not to indulge in something and shames you if you do. But it's also the voice that encourages you to indulge. The ego is both the controlling judge and the tempter. It causes the problem by encouraging indulgence, it keeps the problem in place through addiction and shame, it offers solutions to the problem, and then sabotages those solutions with more temptation and shame.

When Alcoholics Anonymous asks people to surrender to a higher power, they aren't asking people to surrender their true power and will, but their small will. AA does this because they realize that the small will, the will of the false self, is part of the problem, not part of the solution. In asking people to surrender, all that's being asked of them is to give up the struggle against life, to give up the desire for life and for themselves and others to be different. This rejection of what *is*, is the small will opposing life. It is the ego. Such rejection of life is the essential error, or misunderstanding within humanity, which needs to be healed and is healed by Presence.

Emotional issues, which are at the root of addiction, stem from feelings created by the ego's resistance to life and the refusal to accept what has happened. For example, anger, sadness, regret, resentment, hatred, and blame come from essentially the same misunderstanding, the same wrong-minded declaration: "That should not have happened!" This simple, yet life-altering, misperception is the origin of the emotions that drive addiction and keep it in place. Uncovering this lie at the heart of one's emotional life and surrendering it — letting this belief go — is central to recovery.

You are not the self that is addicted and has mistaken beliefs and emotional wounds, but what is able to see these and heal them with compassion and awareness. The divine self is the self that heals the false self, and none other. How could the false self ever heal itself, and why would it want to? The ego doesn't want you to discover your divine self because then the game would be over; the ego would be ousted from its position. But how is the divine self inserted into this situation, especially when someone is in a deep state of en-darkenment?

The only way out, as they say, is in. The way out of the emotional pain underlying addiction is by going into that pain.

This is done, not by reliving the pain as your human self, but by bringing the light of Presence, or awareness, to whatever had been rejected because it was too painful to experience at the time. You start by just being willing to look at and sit with any difficult emotions that come up in your life.

The way to uncover past pain and heal it is to be with current pain. By being present to whatever painful emotions are currently arising, you are bringing Presence to your emotional self, including all the stored emotions from the past. You are saying to your unconscious: "I'm willing to acknowledge and experience my emotions." This is a very different message than is usually delivered to the unconscious.

When the unconscious receives this message, it releases information into your conscious mind in the form of images and insights that will help you heal. The emotion that is being healed is connected to many other moments when you felt that same emotion, perhaps even for the same reason. So when you sit with an emotion to heal it, you're also healing it in other moments when you weren't willing to sit with it. Presence heals retroactively.

As you sit with an emotion, the thoughts that fueled it, both currently and in the past, will be uncovered. You'll see that you believed many thoughts that weren't true and how those thoughts created those feelings. Such mistaken beliefs are innocent enough, and you can forgive yourself for them. Forgive yourself for having an ego that comes to false conclusions and gets hurt and angry over its own conclusions. Have compassion for the human self that doesn't know any better way to deal with life. But you, as the divine self, do know a better way, as you sit in Presence with the human self.

You may argue that you don't know how to be in Presence with your emotions, but fortunately, you would be wrong.

Everyone can do this. You don't have to have a certain level of spiritual mastery to be present. Everyone knows how to be present; they just don't usually choose to be. Consciously choosing to be present to an emotion is a very powerful act.

When you are willing to be present to an emotion and you choose to do this, what is doing this is Presence. You are already there, in Presence, once you make the commitment to sit with an emotion. The willingness *is* Presence. And how hard is it to sit with something? Sitting with something is just being with it and noticing it. It's letting everything be as it is and then noticing how what *is,* is revealing itself in new ways.

When you sit with something, that something is always changing, whether it is the sky, a body, your dog, a sound, a tree, a sensation, a thought, or a feeling. All of life is in constant motion. The emotion you sat with when you started is not the same emotion you're sitting with minutes or even seconds later. This flow of change, of life, is what you give your attention to. Your attention has to be this close, this intimately involved with what is.

Get curious, just look, and be willing to see what's there. What is this mysterious thing called anger or sadness or disgust? This giving of your attention, of Presence, heals. It does this in part by revealing something, but attention itself is healing in a mysterious and inexplicable way.

There are two aspects to healing a bad habit or addiction. The first is what was just mentioned: Heal the feelings that drive the addiction. Give your attention, acceptance, and compassion to any difficult feelings that arise in your life. These feelings are an inroad to other feelings that might also need attention, including ones that have been buried. Sit with whatever you're feeling, let those feelings be as they are, experience them, and investigate them, and in this way heal them.

The second aspect of healing a bad habit or addiction is bringing awareness to the urge to indulge in it when that arises. Bring Presence—the light of awareness—to the mechanics of desire. When you feel the urge to reach for those cookies, that cigarette, that drink, that credit card, or that drug, stop and look to see what's going on within you. Get curious about that urge: What does that feel like? Where do you feel it? If it had a color what would it be? If it had a voice, what would it say? Sit with that urge, experience it, explore it, and listen to it. What are the thoughts behind it? How does it convince you to follow through?

It is Presence that does this looking and only Presence that's willing to be with whatever is going on. When you stop even for just a moment and give your attention to what's going on inside you rather than unconsciously move towards the desired object, as your ego would have you do, something very important happens: Space is created around that urge. Within that space is the possibility of making a choice other than the usual one.

Anytime you choose to not indulge in the usual choice, the habit or addiction is undermined, weakened. Every choice in that direction matters. Those choices add up and make the next choice easier. They also demonstrate that there's something else here—your divine self—that can choose differently.

When you are completely identified with the egoic self, it feels like you have no choice. You're at the mercy of your desire. You believe you need whatever it is you want, or you'll be missing something. If you can stop a moment, however, take a breath, and notice if Presence is available even in that desire-laden moment, you'll be able to see that there are other possibilities. Stopping, taking a few deep breaths, noticing what is going on within you, being with the urge, and exploring it are all means of bringing more Presence into the moment and, along with it, choice.

Once you realize you have a choice, you can replace the old choice with a healthier one. Breaking a habit is much easier if you replace it with something rather than trying to *not* do something. By replacing the old habit with something different, what you're actually doing is creating a new, healthier habit. That new habit will eventually feel as normal and fulfilling as the old habit did. Some simple examples are replacing coffee with tea, smoking with chewing gum, or eating sweets with eating fruit.

When you try to *not* do something, however, the experience is one of lack. You imagine yourself doing what you'd like to do, which makes you want to do it. You feel like you're missing out on something if you don't do it. But you aren't. There have been so many other moments when you didn't miss that object of desire a bit.

What makes a moment of desire so powerful, so compelling? Why does an urge feel, at times, so irresistible? The answer isn't really so mysterious: If you've responded to a desire repeatedly in the past, your brain has been trained to desire it. Initially, the desire, itself, convinces you of the need for something. Desire is a thought that has an emotionally-based sense of need attached to it. If that desire is thought about or fulfilled repeatedly, it grows in intensity. However, if it isn't thought about or fulfilled, it will fade away. There are lots and lots of things you don't desire because you don't think about wanting those things.

If you have a habit or addiction you want to break, you have to un-train your brain by not thinking about the object of desire and by not pursuing that urge. It takes consistency over time to extinguish a desire, but essentially that is all that's entailed in breaking a habit or addiction. When it comes to desire, humans are no different than lab rats: Behaviors that are reinforced continue, and ones that aren't do not.

There is nothing inherently meaningful or special about any desire. Your favorite desires are simply thoughts you've thought and responded to many, many times. And that's all. Your desires don't hold the key to your personal happiness. They don't improve your life, and indulging in them certainly doesn't. The little bit of pleasure you receive from them quickly passes. Your rational mind can see this, but because desire comes from the irrational part of the mind, you have to bring a lot of awareness to your desires to overcome them.

If you can get beyond that moment when the urge feels the strongest, you'll discover that the urge naturally dissipates, just as any thought or feeling does when it isn't fed. Being present to the experience of the urge allows you to see it for what it is. It is just an urge, it isn't meaningful, and it will soon disappear. Any idea that fulfilling your desire will make you happy is an illusion, a misunderstanding. Presence can help you see the lie that is desire. The simple awareness that is Presence can heal any area of your life and make more room for the divine self to live as you.

CONCLUSION

As soon as you think or say "I," the character comes to life. How much ego is expressed by that character in that moment depends on how much you are identified with "I." There might be only the slightest bit of ego, just enough to function and interact with others. Like wisps that form briefly into a cloud and then dissipate, you might identify with "I" only very briefly and slightly, while you remain seated in Presence. Or something very different might occur: You might believe what you're saying completely—you believe you *are* the character—in which case, you have either lost Presence temporarily or never really found it. These are the two extremes: the fully enlightened mind and the mind caught in illusion.

There is another possibility in between these extremes: You might *notice* the character believing, at least to some extent, what the character is saying. You are involved in the play as the character, but not completely. You have one foot in the human self and one foot in the divine self. What notices the character playacting is the divine self. Some Presence is available to the character, and that changes everything. The degree to which Presence is available to the character is the degree to which the character is enlightened. Presence *is* the light of consciousness. It brings the light of awareness to the darkness of the illusion of a separate self, the illusion that you are an independent character.

These possibilities relate to four stages in spiritual development. In the first stage, you only know yourself as the character. You believe that's who you are and don't even think of questioning this. In this stage, the ego is mostly in charge of the character and the character's life, or at least trying to be. There is no awareness on the part of the character of any other possibility.

In the second stage, the experience is one of going back and forth between believing you are the character and experiencing Presence. Through meditation and other spiritual practices or through Grace, you've discovered Presence, but you still don't know yourself *as* Presence. Presence is an experience the character has during meditation, on walks in nature, or while drumming or dancing, for example, but Presence seems to come and go. After these glimpses of your true nature, which might even be lengthy, you always return to feeling like you are the character. Your consciousness is still seated in the false self. This is the experience of most spiritual seekers, which they often describe as having "got it" and then "lost it."

The third stage, which is the result of self-realization, or awakening, is knowing yourself *as* Presence. In this stage, your consciousness is fully seated in Presence, while at times, noticing yourself identifying with the character to some extent. You occasionally may become very involved in playing the part of your character, including having feelings. But even then, you never lose sight of the fact that you are playacting. Your words and even your feelings can feel oddly like they aren't real or not yours; and yet, you speak them and go through the motions of being this character. You are simultaneously aware of watching the play of life and participating as the character you are playing.

At this point, the degree to which the character suffers or causes suffering to others is the degree to which the personality has not been purified of ego and the wounds caused by the ego. If the psychological issues and wounds are mostly healed, being the character isn't likely to cause much suffering. The divine self will shine through quite purely. On the other hand, if those wounds are not healed, this character will still experience some suffering and cause suffering to others. For instance, if some fear still exists in that character due to childhood abuse, then under certain circumstances, anger and other emotions will get triggered as defense mechanisms.

This explains how some people can be self-realized but still not be so happy or free of emotions or difficulty in relationships. Someone can be self-realized but still have a lot of healing to do, in which case the character's behavior will not appear all that enlightened. You are only as free of emotions as you are healed.

The same unhealed person might still be able to transmit Presence very powerfully to people while in the role of spiritual teacher. Once one is self-realized, the capacity to be a pure channel of Presence is there and, in the right circumstances, can be actualized. However, in more ordinary circumstances, especially when that person is under stress or challenged by others, any remaining wounding is likely to compromise that purity.

The fourth stage is full enlightenment, which is quite rare. Many who've reached this stage are no longer participating in the world very much. They've gone through the various stages and completed the human journey and are spending much of their time in other dimensions, absorbed in meditation. Many of these individuals are unknown to the world, although some have disciples. Such individuals may have spent most of their life in a state of enlightenment and reclusion or only part of it. This stage is not to be confused with the unintegrated state, which is one of incomplete realization and escape from the world. On the other hand, this last stage might also be lived very much like the third stage.

The journey from self-realization to full enlightenment can be a very long one and is often not completed in one lifetime. The more awareness brought to any remaining mistaken ideas and unmet feelings, the more quickly this evolutionary process proceeds. This clearing of the clouds is essentially the work of enlightenment, both before self-realization and after.

Although clearing the clouds that obscure blue-sky consciousness continues even after self-realization, that work is much easier once you are established in Presence, since Presence does all the work. From Presence, there is a natural curiosity about whatever is happening and no resistance to seeing the truth about thoughts and feelings, and the truth can be seen more quickly. Even when identification happens and emotions arise, Presence notices this. Slowly, all of this noticing chips away at the egoic lies and unconscious material that continue to arise, until there is very little left to heal. The result is an individual who is both completely at home in his or her humanity and in the world, but not of it.

This is the journey you are on, and it is all good, all designed especially for you, by you. When you finally come to the end, what it was all about becomes crystal clear, and you rejoice in the magnificence of such a plan. The preciousness of the human drama is finally apparent, and all you can do is bow deeply to it and take your own bows for playing your part so well.

ABOUT the AUTHOR

Gina Lake is a nondual spiritual teacher and the author of over twenty books about awakening to one's true nature. She is also a gifted intuitive and channel with a master's degree in Counseling Psychology and over twenty-five years' experience supporting people in their spiritual growth. In 2012, Jesus began dictating books through her. These teachings from Jesus are based on universal truth, not on any religion. Her website offers information about her books and online course, a free ebook, a blog, and audio and video recordings:

www.RadicalHappiness.com

If you enjoyed this book, we think you will also enjoy these other books from Jesus by Gina Lake...

Jesus Speaking: On Falling in Love with Life: This audiobook is Jesus speaking from another dimension today. His message, as channeled through Gina Lake, is meant to bring you into greater alignment with the Christ within you, with Christ Consciousness. It is also intended to give you the experience of having a relationship with the wise and gentle being we've known as Jesus the Christ, as he speaks to you as if you were sitting in his presence. In it, you will discover how to become the loving, strong, and peaceful being you are meant to be, which Jesus exemplified. 5 hours.

Available at:

www.radicalhappiness.com/audio-video/jesus-channelings

The Jesus Trilogy. In this trilogy by Jesus, are three jewels, each shining in its own way and illuminating the same truth: You are not only human but divine, and you are meant to flourish and love one another. In words that are for today, Jesus speaks intimately and directly to the reader of the secrets to peace, love, and happiness. He explains the deepest of all mysteries: who you are and how you can live as he taught long ago. The three books in *The Jesus Trilogy* were dictated to Gina Lake by Jesus and include *Choice and Will, Love and Surrender,* and *Beliefs, Emotions, and the Creation of Reality.*

Awakening Now Online Course

It's time to start living what you've been reading about. Are you interested in delving more deeply into the teachings in Gina Lake's books, receiving ongoing support for waking up, and experiencing the power of Christ Consciousness transmissions? You'll find that and much more in the Awakening Now online course:

This course was created for your awakening. The methods presented are powerful companions on the path to enlightenment and true happiness. Awakening Now will help you experience life through fresh eyes and discover the delight of truly being alive. This 100-day inner workout is packed with both time-honored and original practices that will pull the rug out from under your ego and wake you up. You'll immerse yourself in materials, practices, guided meditations, and inquiries that will transform your consciousness. And in video webinars, you'll receive transmissions of Christ Consciousness. These transmissions are a direct current of love and healing that will accelerate your evolution and help you break through to a new level of being. By the end of 100 days, you will have developed new habits and ways of being that will result in being more richly alive and present and greater joy and equanimity.

www.RadicalHappiness.com/online-courses

More Books by Gina Lake

Available in paperback, ebook, and audiobook formats.

A Heroic Life: New Teachings from Jesus on the Human Journey. The hero's journey—this human life—is a search for the greatest treasure of all: the gifts of your true nature. These gifts are your birthright, but they have been hidden from you, kept from you by the dragon: the ego. These gifts are the wisdom, love, peace, courage, strength, and joy that reside at your core. *A Heroic Life* shows you how to overcome the ego's false beliefs and face the ego's fears. It provides you with both a perspective and a map to help you successfully and happily navigate life's challenges and live heroically. This book is another in a series of books dictated to Gina Lake by Jesus.

Embracing the Now: Finding Peace and Happiness in What Is. The Now—this moment—is the true source of happiness and peace and the key to living a fulfilled and meaningful life. *Embracing the Now* is a collection of essays that can serve as daily reminders of the deepest truths. Full of clear insight and wisdom, *Embracing the Now* explains how the mind keeps us from being in the moment, how to move into the Now and stay there, and what living from the Now is like. It also explains how to overcome stumbling blocks to being in the Now, such as fears, doubts, misunderstandings, judgments, distrust of life, desires, and other conditioned ideas that are behind human suffering.

All Grace: New Teachings from Jesus on the Truth About Life. Grace is the mysterious and unseen movement of God upon creation, which is motivated by love and indistinct from love. *All Grace* was given to Gina Lake by Jesus and represents his wisdom and understanding of life. It is about the magnificent and incomprehensible force behind life, which created life, sustains it, and operates within it as you and me and all of creation. *All Grace* is full of profound and life-changing truth.

From Stress to Stillness: Tools for Inner Peace. Most stress is created by how we think about things. *From Stress to Stillness* will help you to examine what you are thinking and change your relationship to your thoughts so that they no longer result in stress. Drawing from the wisdom traditions, psychology, New Thought, and the author's own experience as a spiritual teacher and counselor, *From Stress to Stillness* offers many practices and suggestions that will lead to greater peace and equanimity, even in a busy and stress-filled world.

The Jesus Trilogy. In this trilogy by Jesus, are three jewels, each shining in its own way and illuminating the same truth: You are not only human but divine, and you are meant to flourish and love one another. In words that are for today, Jesus speaks intimately and directly to the reader of the secrets to peace, love, and happiness. He explains the deepest of all mysteries: who you are and how you can live as he taught long ago. The three books in *The Jesus Trilogy* were dictated to Gina Lake by Jesus and include *Choice and Will, Love and Surrender,* and *Beliefs, Emotions, and the Creation of Reality.*

Radical Happiness: A Guide to Awakening provides the keys to experiencing the happiness that is ever-present and not dependent on circumstances. This happiness comes from realizing that who you think you are is not who you really are. *Radical Happiness* describes the nature of the egoic state of consciousness and how it interferes with happiness, what awakening and enlightenment are, and how to live in the world after awakening.

Living in the Now: How to Live as the Spiritual Being That You Are. The 99 essays in *Living in the Now* will help you realize your true nature and live as that. They answer many questions raised by the spiritual search and offer wisdom on subjects such as fear, anger, happiness, aging, boredom, desire, patience, forgiveness, acceptance, love, commitment, meditation, being present, emotions, trusting your Heart, and many other deep subjects. These essays will help you become more conscious, present, happy, loving, grateful, at peace, and fulfilled.

Return to Essence: How to Be in the Flow and Fulfill Your Life's Purpose describes how to get into the flow and stay there and how to live life from there. Being in the flow and not being in the flow are two very different states. One is dominated by the ego-driven mind, which is the cause of suffering, while the other is the domain of Essence, the Divine within each of us. You are meant to live in the flow. The flow is the experience of Essence—your true self—as it lives life through you and fulfills its purpose for this life.

Getting Free: Moving Beyond Negativity and Limiting Beliefs. To a large extent, healing our conditioning involves changing our relationship to our mind and discovering who we really are. *Getting Free* will help you do that. It will also help you reprogram your mind; clear negative thoughts and self-images; use meditation, prayer, forgiveness, and gratitude; work with spiritual forces to assist healing and clear negativity; and heal entrenched issues from the past.

Choosing Love: Moving from Ego to Essence in Relationships. Having a truly meaningful relationship requires choosing love over your conditioning, that is, your ideas, fantasies, desires, images, and beliefs. *Choosing Love* describes how to move beyond conditioning, judgment, anger, romantic illusions, and differences to the experience of love and oneness with another. It explains how to drop into the core of your Being, where Oneness and love exist, and be with others from there.

Trusting Life: Overcoming the Fear and Beliefs That Block Peace and Happiness. Fear and distrust keep us from living the life we were meant to live, and they are the greatest hurdles to seeing the truth about life—that it is good, abundant, supportive, and potentially joyous. *Trusting Life* is a deep exploration into the mystery of who we are, why we suffer, why we don't trust life, and how to become more trusting. It offers tools for overcoming the fear and beliefs that keep us from falling in love with life.

For more information, please visit the "Books" page at

www.RadicalHappiness.com

Made in the USA
Columbia, SC
13 December 2018